THE RAT RULES

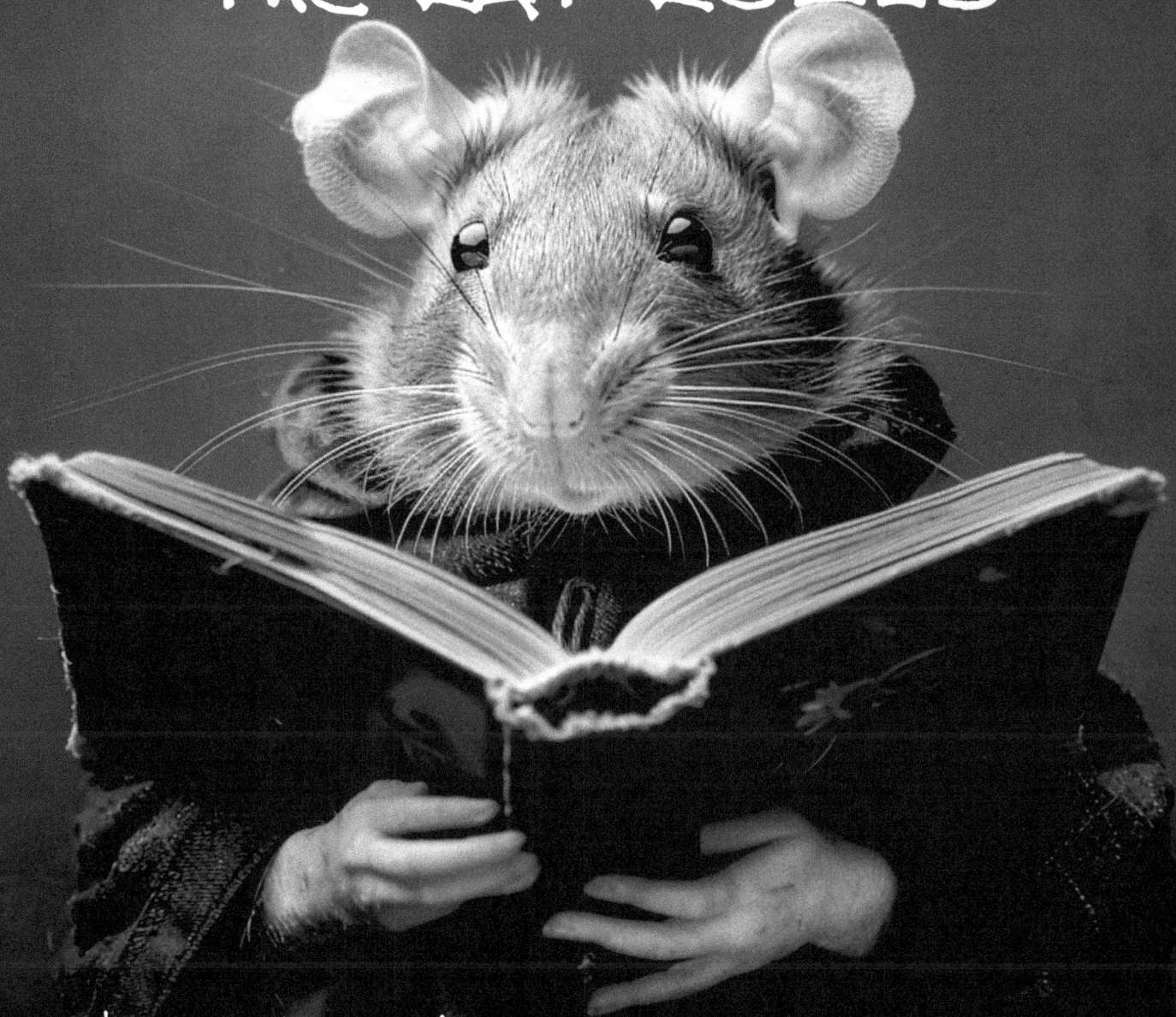

The Secret Way of
the Un-Dammed Life

Ecallaw Leachim

Love says: I am Everything.
Wisdom Says: I am Nothing.
Money says: I have a House in Maui!

A Jewish doctor was being treated very unkindly by his superior in a hospital where he worked. The man asked him, "If I had two bags, one full of wisdom, the other of money. Which one would you take!"
The Jewish doctor did not hesitate, "I would take the money, of course."
The supervisor snorted, "Typical Jew - I would have taken the wisdom."
The doctor smiled broadly and laughed. He looked the man in the eye, saying, "So, we each take what which we do not possess."

Copyright 2024   Ecallaw Leachim
ISBN: 978-0-6452723-7-6
FULL COLOR EDITION

Published by Ladder to the Moon Productions, Australia

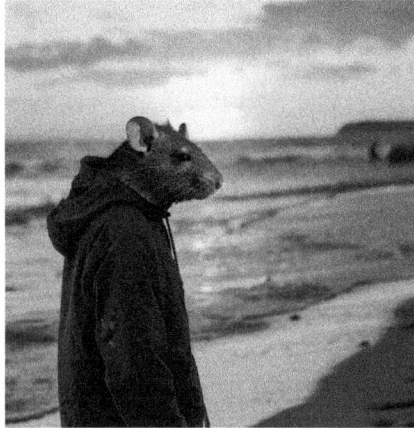

Why Were "The RAT RULES" Written?

Why did I bother writing this book, and who will benefit from it? The short answer is YOU. The long answer: If you practice the simple guidelines, every department of your life will work better. You will make more money, make better friends, and get a better lifestyle. It is a given that most people will WANT this, but it is a fact that the majority do not GET it. Why? What is the difference between a rich man and a poor man?

Everyone wants more money, better relationships, and the respect of their peers. But few achieve this. They fail to see their opportunity, do not catch the tide at its full, and miss out. This book will help you to seize the moment, and as a result, gain greater independence and freedom. And we do this by grasping the simplest thing: *Learn to see the obvious!*

If you are poor, unhappy, feeling lost, it is not fate that decided this, YOU did. Or should I say, the patterns inside our mind project the reality we experience. Little seeds of thought and emotion grow to be whatever it is you experience. The trick is SEEING them!

Once a person sees things clearly, they are put into a position of true choice. Alternatively, when we do NOT see clearly, we are like a person trying to put up a tent during the dark of the moon - We stumble about, stubbing our toes on a hundred small obstacles that appear.

Practising the principles of this book will illuminate your inner vision and bring clarity to your world. It will cut through all the confusions and beliefs that obscure your ability to see clearly. The Rat Rules offer very simple guidelines that will re-frame the very core of your social contracts and allow you to enlarge your world with whatever it is you truly desire.

This is why "The Rat Rules" were written.

Ladder to the Moon
Publishing

Defeating the God of Red Tape

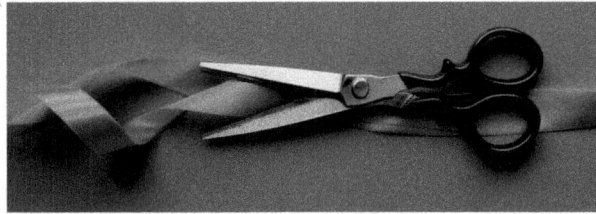

Alex was called in to see the bank manager, as his credit card was way over the limit.

This was a time well before the Internet, before mobile phones. The only security for Credit Cards back then was a list of renegade users. If a store owner caught one, they took the card and cut it – They got a $20 bonus for posting the cut card to the bank. But if you spent under $20 in any single transaction, no one looked up the fraud sheet.

In the 1970's you could do a lot with $20 - fill the car, eat out, pay a cheap hotel bill. My friend lived off his card for eighteen months before the bank finally tracked him down and called him in. He looked very anxious about the meeting.

I explained that the reason they wanted to see him was to cut up his card, in front of him. The shock is supposed to make the offender conform. So he put a series of dashes over the card with a fine point marker, and wrote, "Please cut here".

It worked a charm. When the bank manager demanded his card, and took his scissors to cut it, he saw the dotted line, and squinted as he read the words that were supposed to make him laugh.

He was furious, and shouted at Alex. "You are a CHILD! GROW UP!" The fellow then tried to cut up the card, but he couldn't. It was like he lost his will to act. Instead, he folded it half and threw it into a draw, along with the scissors.

Society controls you by making everything about YOU. Alex was the guilty party. Alex was the foolish child. Alex was the one who needed to cow tow to the rules. The manager wanted to make it all about Alex, but when Alex deferred and just gave him the card with humor, and without guilt or shame, the fellow lost his power.

There is a monster called bureaucracy in our lives. It is full of people that are rigid and humorless, who love to control others with rules – You should do this! You should not do that! Why? Perhaps it gives them a sense of purpose.

The evil creature they worship, the God of Red Tape, is a snake-like beast that attacks all people. Only the bureaucrat appears immune to its venom.

But when you walk with a little humor, when you hold a sense of positive indifference, you push away the controllers beige universe of conformity.

It is like you wear a suit of armor to the battle.

They cannot control you with the rules, and your sincere but friendly indifference means they cannot make you angry - So they let you go.

We defeat Red Tape by knowing the game, understanding the players, and giving it little weight. But first, you have to obey Rule One, and know in your heart that this is not about YOU – it is about them, their rules, and their control.

This truth shall set you free!

INDEX

THE SECRET

It's not what you look at that matters, it is what you see.
Thoreau

Here's a little secret, we all carry a few core issues. These are the source of most of our problems and concerns. This is termed "Core Karma" – these are the seeds from which all our drama and difficulty, as well as all our blessings, grow from.

These seeds are images from childhood that are buried at the heart of our being. But when you are dragging a huge oak cross it is hard to imagine a tiny acorn grew it - That feeling we had as a two year old: Do we even know it still exists?

Karma starts as a picture inside us. Our external reality is like a slide is put into a projector that shows up as a much larger image on a wall.

Good news: The RAT RULES will help you connect your external reality (projection) with the internal cause (karma).

Disconnection is the issue. We do not connect what we see and experience in our life with the seeds within us that have caused them to manifest.

Look at the problem gambler – he/she KNOWS that poker machines are a bad investment. The math says it, logic says it, all your friends will say it, but as a problem gambler YOU cannot see it.

Everyone else knows the poker machines are a dead loss, but YOU, the problem gambler cannot.

All you know is that the odds have to fall your way, eventually - You just have to crack the secret code, the pattern! Blindness to the obvious – We all share it. We all have our 'blind spot'.

There is no pattern, but the companies that make these machines DESIGN them to look like there is. Poker machines are DESIGNED to attract problem gamblers. It is not just the sound and the flashing lights and the small rewards that stimulate brain hormones, it is not even the desire to win: What hooks the problem gambler, what makes them blind to the obvious, is the false belief there is a pattern that can be broken.

But there is no pattern. A poker machine is a random number generator with overall payout's predetermined by a mathematical equation.

It is easy to spot the issue with the gambler, but can you see it in yourself? Where are YOU doing the same thing, over and over, despite the fact you know it is not working? Where are YOU spiraling around an internal seed - a core image or karma - that is whispering in your ear?

Underneath every addiction, every belief, every viewpoint, there is a seed, a CORE KARMA. This is what drove the drove the problem gambler to that casino, to that machine, and which cost them their house, their marriage, and their life.

That is easy to spot, but what is driving YOU?

It is different for each person, but one thing is certain, once we learn the FIRST of the RAT RULES, most of our problems vanish.

That rule is: *It's not about YOU!*

You ask: How could this possibly solve problem gambling? It won't, but once you are released from your fixation, you can more see clearly. This is what solves the problem, seeing things clearly.

Flip this: When it is all about ME I am looking inwards, not outwards. The obvious is staring me in the face, but I am not looking in that direction. The problem gambler sees nothing past their nose. They 'think' they are looking outward, looking for that pattern, but he/she is locked inside his/her belief, looking through a lens that distorts reality.

Blind belief is like living in a bubble. When you are inside a bubble, it becomes a lens you look through, it becomes HOW you perceive the external world. Remember this, it's important.

When you believe it is all about YOU, you are living in a bubble, and you will never see anything clearly. You will never see the seed cause, the causation, that is driving everything in your life.

But step out of the bubble, and everything is clear. It has always been clear, but our self-interest and notions of importance (or insignificance) cloud this clarity, and obfuscate the obvious.

There is a story about a stream that seeks to cross the desert, but it cannot. The sand soaks it up. It cannot make head way. Finally it gives up.

The sun and wind then evaporate the water, thus taking it across the desert as a cloud, where it falls down as rain on the other side.

Our internal seeds of karma are wrapped up in fixations, beliefs, and notions of right and wrong, good and bad, etc. Once we let go of the belief we are the center of the universe, the monkey grip these things have on us starts to weaken.

So, relax. Let the sun and the wind act upon us, allow life to lift us up, and take us to our destiny.

Life WANTS to pick you, to take you to a greater destiny. You just have to let go of your fears, your concerns, and trust the wind.

Seeing the Obvious

The 'core karmas' become visible ONLY when we see the obvious. When we can see with clear eyes, and look at our lives and those around us with a clear vision, it then becomes obvious where the source of difficulties in our world lay hidden.

But: obfuscating the obvious are layers of fear and confusion – this stops us seeing clearly. The Rat Rules allow us to peel back these layers, to remove the crusted debris, and reveal what IS.

Good News! There is a very simple path to seeing the truth, it is called acceptance. When we truly accept our circumstances, the foibles of others, the ups and downs, then we relax inwardly.

Being clever will not help. A small clue: acceptance works best with practicing gratitude, kindness, and courtesy to all you meet.

This brings us acceptance, acceptance releases the monkey grip we have on reality, so now we can embrace this moment. We will not just find our wings but learn to to spread them, and fly free.

Let's find out how!

Inner Knowing

What is the difference between the apprentice and the Master?

How they see!

The Master sees the problem as solved while the apprentice sees a problem to solve.

We have all walked into a café and gone, "Yep!" or "Nope!" We have all experienced the thing I call your RAT, the *Reality Awareness Trigger* - This is the thing that just knows if a situation is good for you, or otherwise.

There is a small voice inside that just knows. Why it knows, or how it knows, who knows? It just knows. Some call it consciousness, others call it intuition, some just think of it as a nebulous Spirit - I call it your spark of survival - a deep aspect to your consciousness that wakes up when either danger or opportunity presents itself.

You might call it instinct, a survival reflex. I call it your RAT, your *Reality Awareness Trigger*. One thing is certain, listening to this inner whisper means you survive better, and live life with far less stress. You may even find happiness.

The RAT is a pun on the RAS. The Reticular Activating System. (RAS) This is a ganglion of nerves that sit in the center of your brain. Its job is to regulate behavioural arousal, consciousness,

and motivation. Yet our RAT is MORE than this. It has a sense of knowing. It is the CONSCIOUS TRIGGER for our survival instinct, and the agent of perception, all rolled into one.

The PROBLEM is hearing this small voice of knowing. In the midst of all the noise inside us: social training, beliefs, notions of right and wrong, what is the true voice? Society shouts you "must" act in certain ways. The inner child tells us to avoid conflict. The emotions tell us to find things that make us happy. The mind says whatever it is programmed to say. And the combination of this gives a gestalt of contradictory notions.

An old friend, Professor George Cockcroft (who wrote the cult classic, "The Diceman") put it simply as: "We are multiple".

So: How do we know our true voice from the echoes of social training? How do we determine the voice of truth from the gaggle of lies?

9

This is the reason for this book: The RAT RULES will guide you to the place where it is easier to discern the correct direction in any circumstance. This is when you start to fall on your feet. This is where you discover your luck. This is where your efforts are rewarded.

How could such a simple notion as, "It's not about you!" make such a difference? It is so simple: When you stop looking at yourself, you start looking at the world. When you look at the world, you find endless opportunity awaits.

When you find CLARITY you start to see opportunity no one else noticed. You use what others call stumbling blocks and build a house with them. And you find doorways open for the courageous few that knock boldly for admission.

It is not the strong that survive; it is the canny, the clever, and the wise. The Rules are designed to teach you these things by helping you come into agreement with your inner RAT. And here is a REAL truth: When aligned to our natural truth, it is remarkable how differently we see things. Further: When we perceive things clearly, all our actions gain greater impetus, power, and respect. You become a person who can JUST DO IT!

HOW We See is Important.

Remember this axiom: *HOW we see is more important than WHAT we see.* Our mind and upbringing may convince us a thing is true, but clarity will reveal this to be patently false.

We once believed the world to be flat and sailors lived in fear of falling off the edge. If you had dared suggest otherwise, you would be thought a fool. Doctors prescribed mercury as medicine and believed you had to bleed a patient to cure them.

These were fixed 'truths', believed with absolute conviction. Any who saw the obvious, and suggested otherwise, was a fool or a lunatic.

This is the thing, seeing clearly will not necessarily make your social world easier, but deep within you will have a sense of certainty. It is the Thoreau quote: *"Any man more right than his neighbors constitutes a majority of one already."*

Yet, this is precisely how a madman thinks! The difference is with clarity of vision.

Once we train our mind to see things clearly, once we learn to observe the obvious, it changes HOW we see everything. The Rules of the Rat are here to show you how to see things in a clear light.

The best thing about the Rat Rules, they are easy to apply, and they work! They are simple, and not difficult to follow. Yet when applied, they turn everything in your life to a net positive. What's not to love? Yet, even so, your old self will resent and object to these changes.

The elephants in the room, the impediments to change, are all the little programs you have running in our head. These often seem large and important, overwhelmingly so in some cases.

We all have religious beliefs, political beliefs, all sorts of beliefs – they may seem big and important things right now - but the Rat Rules will demonstrate how they are tiny things, and help us understand how ALL our cherished opinions, our notions of self, our perception of right and wrong: all these things are our stumbling blocks.

These simple but precise guidelines can take some time to understand, but if you gnaw on what they mean, practice them as best you can, your eyes will be opened to the obvious, and you turn your stumbling blocks into your path.

Why You Need this Book

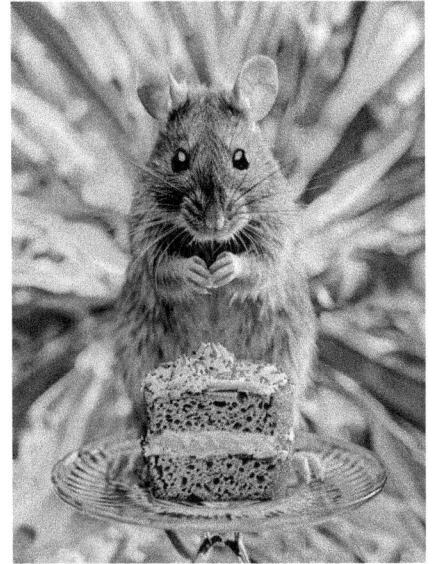

Do you like to have FUN?
Do you want more MONEY?
Do you want be IN CHARGE of your life?
Do you want to have your cake, and eat it too?
Do you desire the RESPECT of your peers?

Then understand and follow the RAT RULES!

I can't promise you respect from others, but your SELF respect will go up when you practice the easy-to-follow guidelines offered in this book. It is so simple, we can summarize the entire book in one sentence: *Learn to see the obvious.*

The problem with the obvious; it is rarely obvious, until it is. It is like those odd images called autostereograms - apparently random patterns that look like nothing until your mind keys in and sees the image locked inside it.

Ideally, we use logic to determine the obvious. In Latin the term is: *Res Ipso Loquitur*, the thing that speaks for itself. But the problem with logic is that so many believe illogical things are logical. These false beliefs are called the "Logical Fallacies" - look them up on Google, you will find you believe in at least one of them.

Pythagoras formed the basis of logic and recognizing the obvious in Ancient Greece with his teaching of mathematics. He used math to prove things, such as the Pythagorean theorem – this was the start of the scientific method, and the modern university system.

Socrates would quiz people. They would make a statement, then by using open questions, he would prove it false. He asked simple, obvious questions, but would do so in such a way that the answers given became the reverse of their statement. This would be obvious to the people watching, but rarely to the person being questioned.

We can all easily see the flaws in others. But I ask: *Why do we so rarely see our own flaws?*

Robbie Burns wrote: *Oh what gift the givee give us, to see ourselves as others see us! T'would from many a blunder free us, and foolish notions:*

We all have our blind spot. We are locked inside our own beliefs and opinions. We cannot see anything but our belief and 'foolish notions".

Yet, apply Rule ONE, "It's not about me!" and we start to see how others might see us!

There is a story of a happy child, everything in his life was rosy. To prepare him for inevitable disappointment, his father locked him in a barn, to try and knock some of the silliness from the boy.

Well, after three days, he opens it up, expecting a weeping lad. Instead, a happy fellow is shovelling aside the horse manure, singing away.

The father is confused, this was meant to be a harsh lesson in life. "Why are you so happy?"

The boy looks up, smiling, "With all this evidence, there has to be a pony in here!"

The GOOD NEWS: There IS a pony in here. The RAT RULES are principles that, when practised, lead you to a clear place where you find clarity and comfort in your life.

In the plethora of self-help and consciousness books, why is this one any better than the others? That's easy – this one works! You don't have to say prayers, you don't need to do yoga, or practice positive thinking - you don't have to do anything other than what you presently do! The only effort you need put in is with HOW you see things.

HOW do you see? From this, all else follows.

Most of us would like our lives to improve in some way, yes? This necessitates a change of some sort. I say we mostly need to change HOW we see things.

Any change, be it a material, emotional, mental, or spiritual, requires a change of viewpoint. If you are needing money, or respect, or anything, HOW you see things will determine everything, and put you into a position of loss or gain.

Core to this study is a statement : *HOW we see is more important than WHAT we see.*

Obviously: Seeing things differently requires a different viewpoint. Change creates a different view, and a different view creates change. The point: Until we change HOW we see things, we will tend to keep seeing everything the same way.

SO! What do I mean by changing HOW we see?

We all know what its like when we fall in love, we only sees the wonderful stuff about a person – but not just that, we are full of energy, we can make love five times a day, we are happy, fulfilled, brimming with confidence.

Then we fall OUT of love, and call all that wonderful state of being a lie.

But if you are in charge of HOW you see, you can sustain this wonderful state of love.

When we focus on HOW we see something, we are living consciously and with purpose - More importantly: We are living with the power of choice. And we soon discover, by choosing HOW we see a thing, we define both it and ourselves.

Our true choice starts with a question: *How do I want to see the thing before me?* If you are asking this question, good news! You are taking charge of your moment.

Merely asking, "What do I want?" is not a choice - It is a shopping list you compile. Good to do, but it changes nothing. Choosing HOW you see something is primary choice - Choosing HOW you see a thing will change your world.

Further, when we take control of HOW we see, it is remarkable how much MORE we will see.

If you wish to see clearly, ask HOW you will see any particular thing. A subtle shift happens: We start seeing the obvious. This is powerful. I cannot tell you when this shift will happen, but I can promise you, practice the Rat Rules, it will.

Make this internal choice, and the world aligns to a new horizon - a better place.

Positive Disinterest

We will come back to this phrase a few times in this book. Finding a positive detachment - being aware yet distant with all that is around us.

When we stop to ask HOW we might see a particular thing we are becoming positively disinterested in what is before us. As a result we start to see more clearly. We are invoking Rule One: *Its not about you.*

The RAT RULES are a very efficient way to see things in a clear light. If we train our mind and emotions to follow them, we will find clarity of vision, our choices will improve, our finances will magically repair themselves, and our sense of freedom will increase.

Let's look at the flip side to this viewpoint: If you are poor, lonely, depressed, or lacking in motivation, it is because of HOW you see things.

This may shock you - but there are no victims. YOU created your problems. HOW you see determines WHAT you experience.

Stumbling Blocks

Getting to clear ground means climbing over the debris in our path. Our stumbling blocks are traps inside us, hidden in plain sight: Self doubt, false belief, religious fear, etc. A clue: Right or wrong, are neither right nor wrong - they are viewpoints.

If we can stop seeing in terms of right or wrong, and start seeing in terms of useful or not, we start to thrive. Equally, when we start using common sense as our yardstick, our burdens lessen.

Freedom can be yours! Even better: When we apply the RAT RULES, we stop living with regrets, and start laughing with options.

So, I wrote this book called "Un-Dammed" – it is a path to clear out the clutter that is damming you up inside. It is Book One of the Ratology series –This series of books inspect the detailed core of who and what we are, and offer ways to heal and grow through adversity. All is wrapped around a simple set of guidelines included in this book: "The RAT RULES".

Everything improves in our world when we understand and follow these guidelines. However, there are always hurdles in our path. Before we can truly be free, be our true selves, first we all have to weave a path through the stones in front of us – We must navigate the maze of our society and our upbringing.

Let's look at this.

The MAZE

"The future is an ever-shifting maze of possibilities until it becomes the present"
Terry Brooks

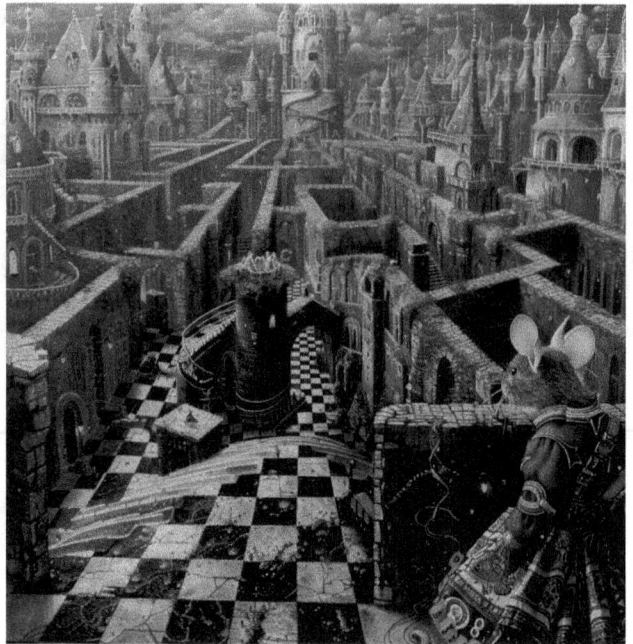

Babies are cute little suckers. They look at you with those bright eyes and gurgle, you have to love them. Same goes with ducklings, kittens, and puppies. Thousands of You Tube videos of them, and they all put a smile on your face.

If everything stopped there, life would be simple. But it doesn't – A baby doesn't stay a baby – the little thing has to suffer the indignity of toilet training, wearing clothes, going to school, and learning to fit in. Then comes puberty, with all its complication: relationships, jobs, all the things that load us down with worry and concern.

We have our brief interludes of light: when we fall in love, when things go right, when we win the football match. But mostly, our lives are spent trying to find a way through the maze of pressure: to conform, to succeed, to be the ideal partner, etc.

But we can all agree babies are cute, yes? At least ONE thing remains uncomplicated in life.

Apparently not: Here come the scientists, asking WHY babies were cute. A study in 2016 asked WHY babies are cute. Why even ASK this question? What is there to understand? Babies are cute, everyone loves them: Just leave it alone.

As if things are not complicated enough, someone gets funding to make it worse.

I love the insane commentary about the study: *Professor Kringelbach said: 'This is the first evidence of its kind to show that cuteness helps infants to survive by eliciting caregiving, which cannot be reduced to simple, instinctual behaviours. Instead, caregiving involves a complex choreography of slow, careful, deliberate, and long-lasting prosocial behaviors,*

14

which ignite fundamental brain pleasure systems that are also engaged when eating food or listening to music, and always involve pleasant experiences.'

Oh PLEASE! What a load of utter crap. What a waste of intelligence and time, asking why babies are cute. Everyone knows they are, but to suppose this is 'calculated' by babies is just insanity.

They are BABIES! B A B I E S!

Welcome to the MAZE. This is the nonsense that builds the maze of confusion we have to somehow find our way through in this life. Bored scientists, who cannot see the obvious, rationalize that cute is DESIGNED by babies to ensure they get what they need. Seriously? Do we really imagine a baby CALCULATED being cute? It is a like saying someone is cool because they designed themselves to be cool – which is very uncool.

Sophistry like this is not new. People find a hole in their life, and proceed to fill it with space. Yet keep in mind, someone is giving out GRANTS to research this! This means other people have agreed with them - so there is a collective stupidity that runs far up the chain.

If a person knew and applied the RAT RULES, so much time and money would be saved. These rules echo the obvious - they grant you common sense, which helps you cut away the crap and get to the facts.

So: Is cute a SURVIVAL tactic designed by babies? No, you misunderstand, say the scientists. EVOLUTION provided this facility by ensuring only the cute babies survived.

So: Is that to say the other ones got tossed in a river, because they were not cute enough?

Give me a break. Intelligent stupidity like this is rampant. It is a disease stalking the halls of universities, and it is ALL based around an inability to perceive the obvious.

While I scoff, I do understand that the study involved looking at the effect of cuteness on the mother and those around the child. But rather than rationalize cuteness, why not accept this as a start point for humanity?

Let's flip this. Let's look at life from a baby viewpoint. For one, babies do not possess hate, or lust, or suffer bitterness. They aren't depressed, and if loved and cared for they are not anxious.

Yet as they learn to walk and talk, and start to navigate the Maze of Life, some babies start to lose the 'cute' and pick up these negative states of mind – while others do not. Why is that?

Obviously, our environment teaches us. So, if you have an angry parent, you learn about anger. Or do you? What, exactly, do we learn?

Have you ever wondered about this? Sure, our environment teaches us, but we each respond to this in different ways.

I look at people's thoughts and emotions like the signals sent from a radio station. Their children are the radios that pick up the signal, and depending on what they tune into, this is the song they will record and eventually sing. Except, it is not as simple as this. Some children have violent, angry parents; yet grow up without a hint of this in their lives. Or so it may seem.

The song we listen to DOES have an effect. While the song itself changes, the mental images and emotions the parents and peer groups send out get lodged in the subconscious of each child.

It could be anger that was taught, it might be repression, fear, anxiety – the child takes it in. It osmoses into the psyche like a popular song, but it is the **reaction** to that song that is the emotion that is expressed. Something to contemplate: *An angry person is playing a song from the soundtrack of emotions they learned as a child.*

But we can choose to sing a different song.

How? By gaining the ability to change how we see things. Choosing HOW you see things is like lifting the record needle off where it has been stuck, and choosing what music you will play. By doing so, we improve our chances to see things clearly. Expanding our viewpoint allows a better perception of facts and this enhances survival.

This is the great, defining concept of this book.

Discovering CHOICE

I raised my youngest boy pretty much on my own. I got to see directly how we place patterns of thought and emotions over our children. In much the same way as we dress them, we clothe them in the shape of our experience.

My son would play in the yard, and he would notice daddy under the car, fixing it. Now, this was not something I enjoyed doing. I tended to get angry and hit the thing with the tools. Yes, I knew it was stupid, that it served no purpose, but I felt a little better expressing that I hated not being able to afford a mechanic, and that being under cars with grease over me was not a lot of fun.

Was this how my youngest son saw it. Not at all. He saw me doing grown-up 'man things'. He saw my performance as part of being a man! The message inserted into the child mind was: *Being a man meant getting angry and hitting things*.

Now, I was unaware I was teaching him this until he was four years old. At four, for no reason, he threw a cup on the floor of our house.

My first reaction was to say, "Stop that!" but I caught myself – there was a REASON he was doing this. But what? Then I saw it, me under the car, hitting it, cursing it, and expressing anger. I picked him up, and apologized. "I know I would hit the car when working on it, and get angry. I am sorry that I taught you this, it was wrong of me. I would appreciate it if you didn't throw things about."

To this day, this child remains remarkably calm in the face of adversity, and rarely has any overt display of anger. But let us flip to the OTHER side, and consider if I had gotten cross at him for getting angry – Angry parent getting angry over child getting angry? Catch 22.

THIS is where the Maze begins to grow. This is the start of the confusion. THIS is core karma, the vulnerable garden where the seeds of a dysfunctional adult are planted.

The Cost of Negative Perception

Almost ALL our problems start with a negative perception of reality. These seeds are planted in childhood, and almost all are SOLVED with the right perception of what is before us.

Most of us have been planted with dysfunctional seeds, and a garden of wrong thinking has grown from this. It is time to change - The RAT RULES put us in the position of being able to choose a new path – they help us recognize our wrong thinking and show us how to weed the garden full of compromise and indoctrination.

As I wrote this I was thrown back to a time: years before, when I was standing with my father in a mechanics workshop. Next door echoed with shouting. Someone was swearing and hitting things. I asked the mechanic, "What is that?"

The old mechanic just laughed, "That is the sound of the car winning!" He continued, "An amateur rented the space to work on a car, but he's losing. A real mechanic knows he will win."

BOOM – hit me between the eyes. Getting angry is admitting the situation before you is beating you. Again: *HOW you see is more important than WHAT you see.* In any situation where you know you are in charge, you don't get angry. It does not matter what the situation is, HOW you see yourself and your situation determines how you will act, or react.

The Thai people see a public display of anger with a deep shame. When a person is not able to contain their emotions, they feel shame for YOU. Imagine that you saw anger being expressed as a personal failure. Imagine viewing your anger as an inability to master your moment.

Maybe stop and ask yourself: *Have I ever gotten angry when I felt in charge of everything?*

It is almost impossible to feel anger when you are confident and in control of your moment. Most can accept this. But, why do I say that choosing HOW we see helps determine our reality?

For one, you are choosing. Choice makes you a CAUSE, not an effect. It prevents you from being a victim. If you are choosing how you see, you are no longer helpless, you are not floating on the tides of chance. The simple act of choosing how you see things means you are not just seeing the path, you are actively building it!

The Salvation Paradox

People look for a Messiah, someone to perform a miracle and solve their life. Or they seek an authority figure to approve them. Or they pray to an unseen God to be saved! From what?

Themselves, mostly. But if you can spot and resolve your core karma, you no longer need a savior, do you? It is the Salvation Paradox. *If you can save yourself, there is no need to be saved.*

Begging for salvation is shouting out to the universe that you are incompetent. Start praying for SOLVE-ation, the ability to solve your issues by learning to see a path through the Maze.

And when you start to master how you see things, you quickly understand, everything in your life is here BECAUSE of how you see things.

You are feeling anger? Change HOW you see things: Anger was never the problem: You just needed to be more in charge of your environment.

It is the mechanic story: a person in charge of their world finds anger pointless. We are told to cure anger with patience and perseverance. True, but these virtues are natural and easy to practice when you feel in charge of your world.

Are we getting the thread I am weaving here?

We all have moments of frustration and anger. But when you see the emotion of anger in the light of you not being in charge, your anger will rapidly evaporate. Why? Because now you KNOW the cause, and you know it is a choice. You KNOW when you are back in charge of your moment you will no longer need it. Get the message?

It is the same story with fear, attachment, lust, and greed. If you experience these, then you are not in charge of things. It is Spiritual Arithmetic, which is in Book Two: "Who Gives a Rats"

For now, please accept: HOW we see is more important than WHAT we see.

Choosing HOW we see makes us strong.

So: Is being helpless, weak, and unable to look after yourself a justification for getting angry?

When my three month old son wanted to scratch his nose, his hand and arm had no proper motor control, and he slapped himself in the face. I felt his frustration. I could see him scowl.

He wanted to be grown up already! So, I cuddled him, and explained that it takes time to get in charge of a body. He settled down, but the point is, babies are not BORN angry, they learn it.

We may well feel justified in getting angry, but what purpose does it serve? Babies are born happy, for the most part. Every negative emotion, thought, and feeling we have is an add on.

Yet we also learn positive vibes. Love, kindness, and affection are things we presume to be natural, and they are. But, we still have to see or feel it to bring it in as part of our existence.

FACT: *Our problems, fears, and inadequacies grew from some small spark in childhood.*

All our thoughts and emotions are like this; they need to be 'sparked' by our environment. Like Frankenstein, they need to be brought to life.

The difficulty is that we are all growing up into the maze of uncertainty about who we are, what we are, and where we are going. We all learn to find a path through this maze in different ways, mostly by following someone else We are mimics - so who or what are we mimicking?

I learned language, how to walk, and how to behave by following others. But then, at age four, I got stubborn, foolish, and opinionated – I struck out on my own, believing I knew better. At four I rejected religion as a path to follow. At five I rejected school as a path to follow. And yet by twelve I was full of religious and educational indoctrination, and getting the cane every day.

But didn't I consciously CHOOSE the opposite?

It does not matter what we consciously decide our world will OZMOZE into us – we soak up our environment and take on the color and texture it gives us. The perfect cucumber in a pickle jar ends up a pickle. But if we retain our sense of choice, it is like taking a thread into the Labyrinth of the Minotaur – with a sense of CHOICE we can find our way back to our natural state.

The Maze of Becoming in Western Society is pretty well set. How we solve it is not.

The path to adulthood means learning to navigate the social norms and fitting in with the surrounding paradigm. But now we have the tools to rise about our conditioning. These are the RAT RULES: They put CHOICE into your hands.

Choice is like a chainsaw that can cut through what is blocking you, and clear your path.

Finding Freedom by Seeing the Obvious

So much of our life is like living in a maze – we never know what is around the corner, or where it goes. The more hopeful of us pre-suppose there is some sort of end, some sort of purpose to it all, but most never find just what this is.

Society is the Maze. We travel this path, over and over, in many different ways. Parts of the maze seem familiar, but as to the answer, the reason, the purpose for it all? Very few discover any sort of understanding as to why we are here and what we are meant to do in this lifetime.

Yet when you see the obvious, it's like being lifted above the maze – you can easily find the solution – the entrance, the exit – it is all clear. When we learn to see the obvious, what we are really doing is taking our viewpoint OUT of our personal world of opinion, and placing it, without prejudice, on the object we see.

So, how do we learn to see the obvious?

It is the first rule: *It's not about YOU!* Instead of making something about US, we look for the best path to follow. There is a sensible set of steps we can take to improve any situation, but when we are locked in ourselves, taking things personally, we rarely find an answer.

The solution to everything in our lives is, perhaps surprisingly, found when we are not in it. Our life is a maze – only when you step away from it, when you rise above the social training and the ingrained patterns of belief, can you see it for what it is. It really isn't about YOU! Or at least, not the "you" you are at the moment.

Right now, YOU are a trained dog, taught to obey invisible commands of "Should" and "Should Not". We need to take off the leash of upbringing and strike out on our own path. This is the purpose for the RAT RULES – to give you the necessary break from the existing habitual patterns you believe are YOU. You are far more than this, but illusions blind you to the obvious.

The Power of MEMES

The maze of our existence comes from three basic sources – the parents, the peer groups, and social expectations. The things we picked up on our parent's knee are where the core patterns reside. The second is from the peer groups around us – it could be the view of your older brother, the beliefs in the group of kids you grow up with, or that laughing, alcoholic aunt who sees fairies in the garden. All these things shape what is acceptable and how it may be expressed.

How the individual sees life is essentially learned between the ages of zero and twelve.

The third molding force is the impress of society and accepted norms. True or false is not relevant: In the Middle Ages most believed the world was flat and that witches must be burned.

But before all of these, there is the general current that runs in the river of culture we grow up in. THIS is the absolute core of all the other three influences, this is the inheritance of the past – It is the gestalt of MEMES passed down from the earliest forms of our civilization.

A MEME is an essential image that denotes a core pattern. It is a picture handed down through your society of what is right, what is wrong, what is valuable, what is not.

MONEY is a MEME. Way back in Rome someone realized it was easier to write a chit saying that they held "X" amount of gold in their bank. The person holding this piece of paper was guaranteed a certain figure.

With a sufficient reserve held in Rome, you could rent the villa on the water in Athens, get slaves, and have food delivered, whatever you needed. You could carry gold on you, but you might be robbed, so the chit was safer. The Goddess of Wealth in Rome was Moneta, which is where the term money comes from.

And if you doubt we are still ruled by ROME, look to the figure blazoned on the edifice of the Bank of England. It is called "Lady of the Bank of England" but it based on Juno Moneta – the Roman Goddess of Money.

In the West, the MEMES that run our society are mostly the influence of the Romans. These notions were modified by religion, and cultures that were assimilated into the Roman way of life, while some patterns were modulated by the rare genius of individuals like Caesar and Da Vinci.

How many individuals can you name that changed the course of history? In music, Bach, Mozart, and Beethoven. In politics, Henry the Eighth, Queen Victoria, and President Lincoln. In science, Newton and Einstein, perhaps Kant. In the modern day, Steve Jobs and Elon Musk.

Behind these ground breakers there are a many other contributors - individuals who have made great advancements - but who of these can the general population of the West name?

Obviously, the bad guys stand out, Hitler and Mussolini, Lenin and Stalin. Because of these bad ones, the good ones like Churchill rose to make their mark, but there are precious few outstanding individuals that modified the river of civilization.

Here is the secret - ALL the people who have changed society had the power to see the obvious. THIS is what gave them the power and ability to ACT. They saw to the heart of things..

However, we don't need to be a messiah and change the world. We only have to effect change in OUR world. And the best way to pull yourself out of the stream of images you are drowning in, this Samsara as the Vedic teaching calls it, is the simple act of seeing the obvious.

We learn to see the obvious by obeying the RAT RULES. Where did these rules come from? Well, from observing the obvious, obviously – but they also run parallel to some of the earliest principles held by the Romans. As they are objectively the most successful Empire in recent history, it will pay us to look briefly at why.

Moneta - Bank of England, London

I am ROMAN

By flying, I fall
In falling, I am free
To arrive at the place of Being

In a sense, this book started with a very bad accident: I fell from a building, over twenty-one feet , and woke up blind. This proved to be a significant handicap, because when I came to and got up – I hit my head on something and sent myself unconscious once more.

When I came to the next time, I had some vision – but it was tunnel vision, where you only see a postage stamp sized view directly in front of you – I could see the caravan (where I was living while I built the house) and aimed for that.

The words, "Shell Shocked" occurred to me. This is what a person in the trenches of World War One experienced – you knew only one thing, to get back home. I was in dreadful pain, but I aimed for the caravan. Fortunately, there were no snipers picking off the easy targets, so I made it.

After some hours, I came back to consciousness in my camp bed, and managed to call my ex-wife, who duly took me into a hospital.

The doctor there was amazed that nothing was broken, given the twenty-one foot fall, and sent me away with painkillers. The ex-wife kindly put me in a spare bed at her place.

I was unable to get up or move without pain, so I started reading – And what I read changed my life. It was the McCullough books on Rome – I fell into them completely – I was IN Rome, I could feel the pulse of the city, I KNEW this place and I started thinking how it thought – and with this came a fairly extraordinary realization.

A moment of clarity, an extraordinary certainty, struck me. *Every thought, every feeling, every notion I possessed was in someway an inheritance of Rome.*

What? I am a ROMAN?

With shock, I saw that what I thought were MY thoughts were really hand-me-down notions that had their seed in Roman viewpoints.

Nobility, generosity of spirit, altruism: ideals we prize in Western Society – these are ROMAN ideals. Everything I had ever done had a Roman ideal at its heart. I woke up and I saw that I was ROMAN – I looked like a modern westerner, but in thought and deed, I was Roman to the core.

Of course, McCullough was best known for "The Thorn Birds", a romance - And where does this word come from? The term, while directly relating to Old French, *romanz*, derives its origin from *Romanus* - "Of Rome" - the brave Roman beating the world. Etc.

We call a madman a Lunar-tic, do you call a person possessed with the ideals of Rome, a Roman-tic?

We are a culture immersed in ROME, and is this such a bad thing? They were the most successful people of modern history. Yes, they killed and pillaged their way to the top, but that was the standard of the day. It was what it was. For me, it was the church stuff that evolved out of Rome that was the bugbear.

I had been raised in the Roman Catholic Church, educated in Catholic schools, and taught to believe in a way of life that was essentially a hand-me-down from Roman times.

That was when I noticed the failed marriage was to the perfect Roman Wife – Blue eyed, blond, quiet and unassuming, never saying a word out of place, and yet entirely ruthless – And not to put too fine a point on it, the woman was also the *very last living descendant* of the Hemus line – And this line was the very last surviving patrician family from Ancient Rome.

Not just that, they were patrician assassins in Rome. Think about this, I married the very last Roman Patrician in the world. These were the ruling families of Rome, the people who defined the path of modern civilization, and I married the very last one, from the family all others feared.

Brave or foolish? Or perhaps just stupid?

I had noted she used a cupped hand to scrape off the water after a shower. I did the same. It made sense, less water means the towel does not get as wet – but THIS was a direct hand-me-down of the Roman habit of using a tool to scrape off the oil from the public baths.

At this point I had an epiphany: I was a hand-me-down puppet of Rome! What I believed were MY thoughts - were not. They were the echoes of Roman thought, Roman beliefs, and Roman ideals.

I was seeing CORE KARMA! My feelings, my thoughts, my beliefs, these were not MINE! What I thought of as myself was a patchwork quilt of Memes handed down from generation to generation. My habits and ways of doing things, they were not my own – they were things I had picked up and called my own.

However, the AWARENESS of this was mine – uniquely mine. The truth that I now saw, THAT was mine. The deep sense of alienation I felt, THAT was mine. In that moment, I got divorced – not from the former wife, but from my former life.

HOW did this happen? I had a blinding spark of the obvious light up in my heart. I saw the obvious; I saw that which IS, not as I wanted it to be, but AS IT WAS. Inside my heart and mind, the gnawing sense of something I had felt all my life broke through into the light of understanding.

Something triggered my awareness of reality.

A new reality was triggered by this awareness.

My "Reality Awareness Trigger" had been activated in a blinding flash of the obvious.

My Inner RAT had gnawed through all the indoctrination of society and in some sort of miracle, found its way to the light of day.

Hallelujah

When you see the obvious, when you deeply see and feel it in your heart, it is a little like watching a steam iron straightening out crinkled linen – all the twists and bends that were the fabric of our existence vanish, and a smooth, even surface reveals itself. My inner RAT had appeared and NOW I started seeing everything more clearly.

The Ex-wife had left the marriage without warning, leaving me to somehow juggle the finances of many properties, of which she owned some 60%. For the last two years, all I had done was get money from here, to pay someone over there, and I was getting into ever increasing debt to do so. Now I saw the truth!

"You were intending to leave when I had the offer to buy the 250 acres, weren't you?" I asked as a statement. Why was this important? Because the money offered for that property cleared all debt over seven other properties I was paying off.

She had a guilty greyness come over her. I continued, "Which meant, if you had spoken up, all property would have been free and clear, yes?"

Nothing more was said but a deep sense of guilt was removed in that instance. I had somehow blamed myself for the failure of the marriage, for the increasing levels of debt, for everything – Mea Culpa.

Now, I didn't. The anxiety I suffered lifted. HOW I saw my situation changed. I believed I had failed, but it was the shadow of guilt that had confused me – now it fell away. I saw the Core Karma, the central cause!

The truth shall set you free!

I owed her nothing. She owed me nothing. We gave it a go, it failed, NEXT! After years of thinking that maybe she would return, that in some way things would come right – now I saw it for what it was. *I was stuck in Roman Programing*. I took out the scissors and cut the internal strings that bound me to her.

In doing so, I cut the illusions away from my eyes. For the first time, I sincerely and deeply saw the obvious, and it set me free. I still had many problems to solve, but now I could SEE them clearly.

The RAT RULES offer you a path to freedom. If you follow the principles I lay out you will come to a point of immediate and intimate clarity with all things in your life. And paradoxically, these guidelines follow closely on the original concepts of what it meant to be Roman.

What Rome became after Christianity was a very different place to what it was before. Concepts of guilt, unworthiness, fear of some eternal Hell, and a lack of connection to the presence of divinity in our lives – these are Roman Catholic notions.

But the EARLY Romans did not carry this baggage. Let us walk a mile in their sandals, and see what it felt like to be Roman in the truest sense.

And the Obvious shall set you free!

A Picture of ROME

Only in Rome is it possible
to understand Rome.
Goethe

The Romans had multiple Gods and many different cultures. This meant the Romans had lots of festival days and a huge variety of ways to ask the Gods for assistance. But in their hearts, the true Roman only worshipped Luck and Opportunity – These were the Sabine Gods, Fortuna and Ops - the original Gods of the first agricultural people that lived in the area.

The quintessential Roman outlook was to trust their luck and find opportunity. You faced whatever life threw in your direction, and you looked for any luck and opportunity that could get you into a better position.

Then the Etruscans came along and turned Rome from a small provincial village into a city. They built the first aqueducts, created the first walls, and established Rome as a place of trade. But the Sabine's, the original tribe in the district, retained their agricultural Gods and still worshipped Fortuna and Ops. These were the two little wooden figures on the altar inside every Roman home.

Romans looked to themselves and their luck for the chance to get ahead. Everything was based on Luck and Opportunity, the true religion. No matter how many temples were built, Fortuna and Ops remained at the heart of the Roman way of life.

You respected the other Gods, but your prayers were asking them to help you find your luck and opportunity – With luck, they would send you a clue! Every Roman looked for signs, clues, and portents of the right way to go in every situation. This was their curious way to worship the Gods, by paying attention to what they were saying to you via omens and signs.

People call it superstition, but this way of life proved to be very successful. I would suggest to you that paying attention to what life is telling us is NOT superstition, it is a very good way to stay alive. In truth, the Roman's were the epitome of Rule Three: *Keep one eye open.*

Alongside this worship of Luck and Opportunity came the basic belief that life was short, enjoy it while you can. In later years, the power of Rome expanded, and the austerity of the stoics took hold of the Equestrian (middle) classes and the Patrician (upper) class. But the basic Roman Plebe (lower class) had no real thought of inheritance, or carrying on some dynasty. They had no such burden, and were up for whatever was a laugh, or whatever was a good time.

Having fun meant having friends to have fun with. Drinking, partying, and having a good time were essential to a life worth living. Gambling was rife in Rome, so much so that dicing was banned in the city, other than the day of Saturnalia – a sort of Mardi Gras. In the lower classes, life was short and your friends were your wealth, so you kept them close. This helped you to survive in a harsh world.

Romans held survival as a priority – you always looked out for what was coming, and took steps to protect yourself and your family. This meant being always watchful, making sure there were no immediate threats facing you and yours, and if there were, you trusted your instincts to find the way around it.

"Watch out for chariots" is what a Roman mother would say to her kids –The upper classes traveled by chariot, and if you got in their way, you got run over. You had no relief in a court of law, the wealthy just bought the justice they needed. So, you watched out for things like chariots, and got out of their way.

Judges were regularly bought, political appointments were bought, even votes were bought. There gave a general distrust with government and the legal process. These would not protect you other than, as a Roman Citizen, you could not be summarily executed without a trial. That was your only right.

You had to stay awake. You had to be vigilant and be prepared for things going wrong. If you could afford armor and a sword, you had these at the ready in your household. If you couldn't, you had some sort of weapon to hand, in case it was needed. But common sense tells you, unless winning makes a profit worthy of the risk, better to avoid a fight.

And everyone knew, if it stinks there is a reason. If something stinks in your household, you have to find the reason and solve the concern. But if it does not affect you personally, you just avoid it.

We can summarize the Roman Way of Life:

- Luck and Opportunity are your true Gods
- Have as much fun as you can.
- Keep your friends close.
- Survival is a mindset.
- Look out for any immediate threats.
- Listen to your gut.
- Watch out for chariots.
- Do not trust the government or the law to protect you.
- Be prepared for a fight, but avoid it if you can.
- If it stinks, there's a reason.

If these were the only the memes to have come down to our present day, the need for this dialogue would be slight. But in Rome there was one very powerful addition – the Roman Catholic Church.

The Power of Religion

We cannot underestimate the effect this institution has had on the entire Western Culture. In the positive, it planted the seeds for the civilization we now enjoy. Without this church, without all the strange guilt trips and control measures it employed, it is unlikely the West would enjoy the pre-eminent position it does - but remember how it came about!

Rome did a thing no other culture has done – Rome murdered it own Gods! They killed off their pantheon of deities and replaced it with, "The One True God", the Christian one. By this action, religion and state became bound into what became the Roman Catholic Church.

This new religion BANNED all other forms of worship. Its edicts were ENFORCED by the State - The Emperor Justinian founded the Inquisition in the Sixth Century! No more worship of Fortuna and Ops – even having these figures on your altar could have you convicted as a heretic. You now prayed to an unseen God, called yourself unworthy, and practiced the brutal subjugation of any faith not your own.

This institution insinuated itself into the fabric of Roman life, and altered the basic mindset of the people to such a degree that an early Roman was a completely different individual to a latter one.

Guilt, shame, and sin – these BECAME Roman values, and down the centuries these concepts have defined the West. And they all got wrapped up in the most insidious tool to control the mind and emotions of the people: the SHOULD.

You no longer needed an army to control the masses! Instead you placed over the heads of the populace the weight of the SHOULD, and THIS controlled them for you.

The Should – that most persnickety, pernicious, parsimonious, piece of patter.

We would do so much better if the entire concept of SHOULD was eliminated from our mind and heart. If we are to experience our true nature, this lead weight of blame must be discarded from our consciousness.

The Should, and the subsequent should not, are the controllers placed inside us. These 'plug ins' direct our thoughts and actions.

Thus we have the second step in the Rat Rules - Rule Two: *Do not Should in your own nest.*

So, let us show you how to remove this terrible burden from your life. We do this by practicing the RAT RULES.

The RAT RULES

"In a world of Rules, the Golden Rule is that ALL the Rules will change. To be in charge of this eternal shifting tide, we must learn to see the obvious. Perception is everything."
The Lord High Rat

Since ancient times, our minds have grappled with two conflicting impulses: the primal Fight or Flight response. It is straightforward when facing a mammoth, but navigating these instincts becomes considerably more nuanced in human relationships. The dilemma of choice in such interactions can be profoundly complex.

The primal directives of Fight or Flight are ingrained in our brains. Yet, in the context of interpersonal dynamics, clarity eludes us. We yearn for autonomy, to assert our individuality, yet simultaneously crave security within familial bonds. This tension lies at the core of civilization.

Consider Bob the Caveman, longing to hunt mammoths while Sue, his cave-wife, seeks the comfort of a secure dwelling in his absence. She proposes a trade: "Provide safety, and I'll offer acceptance and nurture a family."

Fair trade is no mans loss. Bob sacrifices some freedom for the rewards of companionship and family. As Bob's circle expands, forming a tribe, the dynamics shift towards mutual exchange. Specialization emerges, along with the barter system. However, with increased numbers come heightened conflicts, necessitating the establishment of societal norms.

The earliest rules were straightforward: Do not steal, do not harm your neighbor, do not disrupt communal harmony. These mandates, framed as "You Should Not," were enforced with repercussions for transgressors. Adherence to these rules ensured communal cohesion, as long as collective well-being and common sense guided behavior.

This equilibrium is often absent in our modern world. An illustrative instance lies in the disparity of gun laws, notably in the United States, where access to firearms remains largely unrestricted, contrasting with global trends towards regulation and control.

But inside us, there is a voice that resists control.

Resisting Control

Why do Americans resist any and all movements to control their access to guns? NINETY percent of the US population agree that background checks are necessary, yet if a politician DOES something to change the status quo, out they go!

Why? It is not complicated: Guns represent freedom.

The problem in trying to resolve gun violence in the US is largely based around what is offered as the exchange. *"You don't NEED guns, the police and army will protect you?"* But no, they won't.

This is not a trade the people believe in. And when violence occurs, it only proves that assertion right.

Media blames the gun lobby, the gun lobby blames something else – everyone is ready to level blame – yet no one seems to see the obvious: Mental Illness.

The first accepted mass shooting incident was in 1949 when a mentally ill ex-veteran, Howard Unrah, used a Luger and shot thirteen people. There were rare instances after that, all involving mental illness.

It is not unreasonable to assume psyche issues as a major cause in mass shootings. Yet, in 1988, the level and severity of mass shooting increased dramatically. This was the year Prozac was introduced.

It is not public knowledge, but in the clinical trials for Prozac, the control group reported that 5% of users had an increased desire for self-harm, while a number of those had a significant desire to kill other people.

Nurses tell me that negative side effects from Prozac affect 70% of people using it – A drug that interferes with your mind. Now if you are disturbed, and a drug affects you in such a way that you want to kill other people, and you have access to guns – well, this is not a recipe for a long and happy life. Worth considering?

If people followed the RAT RULES the rash of mass murder in the US would come to an end. How so? When you come to a point of center – you come to your OMPHALOS. In this place, the desire to harm yourself and others no longer exists.

The Omphalos

Your RAT, your Reality Awareness Trigger, is that aspect of your center that just knows. When you walk into a café it is the part that goes, "Maybe not". It is the part of you that senses the red flags in that person you just met. It is the instinctual knowing of right or wrong in any given situation.

How do you GET to this point of knowing? Just follow the rules I outline, and it will come about naturally. Just following the FIRST rule will stop most social problems. Once you understand that nothing is about YOU, that YOU are not special, that YOU are not the most important thing that is – a large percentage of your concerns will vanish. A great deal of mental illness becomes manageable JUST BY GRASPING THIS. How so?

If it is not about YOU, what IS it about? Just asking this question gets you out of the trapped space inside your head. Just understanding it is not about YOU frees you from competition, from needing social standing, from needing approval, from NEEDING in general. And when you need nothing, you are free to breathe in your moment.

Which begs the question: Where is YOUR moment?

Where is your NOW? It is not inside your problems or fears, this much is certain. Most people are submerged in a swamp of social mores, of rights and wrongs, goods and bads. Your Inner RAT calls out, but the sound is deadened by the thousand should's and should not's installed into your internal programming.

The "should" is the enemy of what is natural. The "should" is the enemy of your moment. The "should" is an essential cog in the internal conviction that it is all about you. The "Should' is the HIDDEN saboteur that is ruining your life and happiness.

The RAT RULES will expose your 'shoulds'. They wake you up and protect your best interests, all at the same time. They are easy to learn, simple to practice, and give almost immediate rewards. Once you start to follow them, your life improves.

More than this, as you practice these rules, you will become aware of the degree of programming you are under. Inside your mind and emotions, a thousand notions and ideals have been installed. They are mostly habits, routines that hold little benefit for you.

The Rules will help you find your true self, your still, certain point of beingness – This is your OMPHALOS - the Belly Button of existence.

The Programmed Self

The truths most live are programmed illusions. We have been programmed with the MEMES of society in a very similar way that a programmer uses code to get a computer to do what he wants. Practice the Rules and you will see how much you have been living out the patterns of belief handed to you by your parents and peers. It is even called a CODE of Conduct!

The good news: You can rewrite the operating code, but only when you understand the language of MEMES inside you. And to do this, you need to be able to see the obvious.

In court you are asked: *Do you swear to speak the whole truth and nothing but the truth?* It sounds good, it sounds important – yet the 'truth' is, most people do not know the whole truth. As Jesus said to Pilate, "What is truth?" At best, we have a sliver of it.

The 'truth' is that the majority of us are living a lie, not intentionally, but because of what we have been taught and how we have been raised. We are stamped out in a mold of our parents, peers, and society.

Most do not know their natural self, only their social self, your PROGRAMMED self. As evidence of this: Most people have a haunted sense that they are not 'Good Enough' in some way. This is why they look to external authority for validation. It is why most need approval in some way.

But babies do not possess this habit: It is a PROGRAM installed into your operating system.

As mammals we need to feel part of a group, part of a family. This is normal. But when we fall into peer groups, parental expectations, and social norms, we can lose our sense of individuality. These influences take over our natural sense of connection to self. Our beliefs and expectations get knotted into complex problems that get tied up into the strings that bind.

We might seek to become independent with education. We go to University, get a degree, and as a result get a higher paid job. But the strings still bind.

We get trade tickets, work as a carpenter, and earn a good living as a result, but the strings of peer pressure still bind us.

We still work on the assumptions of right and wrong we were indoctrinated with as children, and while this is good for society (Social norms DO decrease the number of ax wielding maniacs in the streets) it is not good for helping you to know who you truly are.

The STRINGS that BIND are the thousand small beliefs in right and wrong that control our thoughts and actions. These are the SHOULDS and SHOULD NOTS that control us.

These disconnect us from center. They bind us up with rules, and isolate us from our natural state. This leads to confusion and frustration, and trying to escape this is often the true cause of mental illness.

We need is to cut these strings, yet retain a sense of connectedness, a sense that we are OK. Deep down in our bones we want the recognition that we are good enough, worthy, competent, and - most importantly - loved. We can only truly grasp this state when we are free to choose our path.

Snipping the ties that bind: This is where we start LIVING. This is where we start finding the freedom to express ourselves, and with this, a growing state of contentment. Opposing this is dying the death of a thousand cuts. As the strings that bind tighten their grip, we bleed out our individuality, and slowly lose our connection to the inner child that knows.

If we are not truly living, we are slowly dying, and the normal prelude to death is suffering. Obviously, suffering is not a great path to happiness - This should be self-evident, yet the main religion of Western Society worships a man suffering on a cross?

Finding Self

How do we find a sense of one-ness, a gestalt within? Deep down in our heart there is a need for real and lasting joy. It makes sense that enjoying life and having fun is a necessary part of this agenda, yes? The road to being complete, happy, and whole REQUIRES us to have fun. A laugh a day keeps the doctor away, etc. But is there some sort of road map to happiness we can follow?

GOOD NEWS: YES, there IS! We call this roadmap, "The RAT RULES"! Following these provide a path to freedom and a sincere, lasting happiness.

These are the Rules that all true RATS live by.

1. It's not About You
2. Do not Should in your Own Nest
3. Keep One Eye Open
4. Ask no Favors (Do not a beggar nor borrowers be)
5. Keep your Teeth Honed (Be Prepared)
6. Have a Bolt Hole
7. Do not Expose your Vulnerabilities
8. Pay Attention to your Brother's Activity (but not their business)
9. Pick up and Dust Off
10. Shoot the Pope (metaphorically speaking)

If you want to be free internally, you must grasp the intent and purpose of these RAT RULES. The Rules are self-explanatory when you understand them, yet impenetrable puzzles when you do not. So, let's run through the basics and get a better grasp of this.

This is the all-important starting point in the path of becoming Un-Dammed. This is the study of Ratology - the science of being un-dammed. (IE: happy)

It is very important to understand that these rules are recommendations to help us develop clarity - They are not an instruction manual. These are the 'Bones of the Rat' revealed. If you grasp them and apply them to your own life, you will soon understand how powerful these ten simple rules are.

I am not saying you have to obey them. This opposes the principle of becoming *Un-Dammed* - But if you wish to survive and thrive in this world, the practice of these principles will help enormously.

There is nothing to "Process"

Many years ago I was giving an Australian friend (with his new American wife) a lift back from the farm. I pointed out that a leech was on him so, without thinking about it, my friend got out a lighter and burned it off. We were both Australians with bush experience. This was just a day-today event. But his wife then burst into uncontrollable sobbing.

I thought she was a little over the top with it all, but attempted to cheer her up. However, my friend waved me down as if to say, "Let her go." So I did.

She sat in the back seat sobbing and sobbing, wetting the carpets. Finally the woman stopped weeping enough to explain things to me, because I obviously did not understand how things worked in the modern age. "It's OK - I am just processing. It's the whole bug thing here in Australia that has gotten to me." And in a while she was OK. Honestly: SO much effort and emotion over what was a small, passing matter..

If you want to waste a lot of time and energy to 'process' a dead leech, if you want to make little things big, go ahead. But this is an indulgence in emotion, not

a true experience or appreciation of the moment. Here is how it really works: The present moment is always CLEAR. It is always free of 'stuff'. In the present moment there is NOTHING TO PROCESS, only the moment to experience. Our job is to find a way to stay in the moment. This is our only concern.

There is nothing to process! However, as the very desire to 'process' is usually part of what the problem is, we need to look at it. The problem of turning everything into a process is as follows:

1. We try to bring our 'stuff' into our present moment.

2. The moment doesn't want it. Our mind enlarges our focus to solve the issue (be it positive, negative, or neutral) so the problem starts to look BIG

3. We then believe that, because we feel it is BIG, it is important and we have to process it. This is when we usually make the 'big' mistake -

4. We subsequently go down the slippery slope of false logic by believing that 'processing' is part of the experience of this moment.

It is not.

There is the old story of the Linguistics Professor talking to his students, explaining that in different languages a double positive is really a negative, and how a double negative can become a positive. Then he states that, in English, there is NO example of a double positive meaning a negative. A kid at the back of the class goes, "Yeah, sure!" (this being a double positive that means a negative)

The message: *We get so involved with the details of the process that we miss the obvious.*

Yet, there 'are' real things that we need to process. So let's look at real versus imaginary here. Grief is a real process. Suffering can also be a real process, even when self-inflicted. Divorce is a real process - for some it's a great liberation, for others a disaster.

The process of working through events of significance can increase the depth of our being and lead us to appreciate the moment more deeply. But burning off a leech is just not something worthy of a full-on weeping-it-up. Get it? Perspective matters.

Let me repeat this: *Perspective MATTERS!*

Things like grief and loss of a loved one, these we DO need to process, but we already know that the greatest tragedy will pass. These things, while part of the cycle of life, are not part of the eternal NOW.

Remember: Any sense of loss or gain is NOT part of the moment, just another thing we have brought to it. The secret: *This present moment is devoid of consequences, responsibilities, or reward.* All it holds is NOW, and nothing else. This can be extraordinarily difficult to grasp, but if we are to understand our RAT, this is an essential truth.

It is all about gaining clear perspective. We need to digest the food we eat, yes, but the final process of this is (literally) crap. Yes, we need to be rid of our crap, but this does not mean re-eating it.

Gaining Perspective

As a rule, we create our own problems. We carry our personal cross to our own crucifixion. We are all our own judges, executioners, and saviors. In this 'process' we either learn something useful, or we disappear into the process itself.

Usually we cart about way too much crap about and the real 'process' is learning to junk the garbage. With luck, in doing so we will learn something about being a rod for our own back.

I could go on for another book on 'process' but what we are doing here is quickly moving THROUGH this and getting to the reality of being. In other words, sure, have your process. Do your workshops, exercise your right to cry, experience your misery. When you are finished, come back and we will get to something a little more real than your indulgences.

Primarily, if we are to survive well, we need to keep things in perspective. We need to keep clarity and intent to the forefront of our being. The Rat Rules are designed to assist in getting us OUT of this area of processing our stuff. They move us through our life events and direct us into seeing the obvious.

Therefore, the only true process we seriously need to consider is the path to clarity. This brings us to a basic principle of perspective: *If our thoughts and emotions are clear in every situation, we cannot be trapped or confused by them.*

As we go through the Ten Rules, please keep this in mind.

Important Note:

There is an overriding concept we need to look at. Primarily, the notion that we need to 'process' experiences! This is an exercise in wrong thinking. We need to digest the food we eat, yes, but the final process of this is (literally) crap! Yes, we need to be rid of our crap, but this does not mean re-eating it.

ONE:
It's Not About You

If we want to be free of all the 'stuff' from our past, we must start each day with a clean slate and a fresh heart. But how? If we want to find this state of being, we must understand and apply Rule Number ONE: *It's not about YOU.*

The Paradox: By ceasing to make everything about self, we see what is around us more clearly. We stop looking at ourselves, we stop looking inside, and start looking outward. This is the ONLY WAY to see the truth in all things. Rule One: You are not the most important person in the room - it is not about you!

This is contrary to what most people believe. We are taught it is all about you! YOU are the one to make it happen! YOU are the one to drive things forward! YOU are the only one who can make the difference! This is true, the individual is the person to move things forward, but what happens AFTER success or failure?

Usually, we fall into depression and anxiety. Why? Centrist thinking prevents us seeing past the barrier of self. If it is all about YOU, you can't see past your nose. Win or lose, you lose happiness.

The truth is, very little in our world is really about US – The sun doesn't rise for you, the moon does not shine on your lake alone, the world does not revolve around YOU. And yet, at this same moment, it is all here FOR you!

Let me clarify this: You have a choice to make as you walk through this world: Is your life about NOW, or is it about YOU? Your decision determines whether you struggle in chains or walk in freedom.

Here is the full story of this rule:

1. It's not about YOU.
2. It's not about ME.
3. It's not about US, or WE, or THEM.
4. It's about being alive and experiencing life.

Life is for Living. When you are truly living, you discover you are not that concerned about yourself.

Why? You are too busy living – therefore, you are not watching yourself! Be as a little child – play in the sandpit of life, moment to moment. The child is not worried about what others think, how they look, or if they are late for an appointment.

It's not about YOU, so stop looking at yourself. Stop thinking it is about you.

Why is this important? Not only does the watched pot never boil, if we are always looking at ourselves we are not looking at the world. It is NOT about you! When we understand this, we look outwards - We put our focus on what is NOW.

It is about NOW, not you. It is about you living your life, not watching it.

An old Italian story speaks of a man growing up in his village. At age Twenty, he is full of fire, and does whatever he wants, despite the fact that everyone is watching. At age Forty, he is far more circumspect and careful in his dealings, because he knows everyone is watching. By age Sixty, the man finally sees the truth - no one was ever watching. The COMMUNITY is important, but it is not about you, specifically.

We are all part of a greater experience called life.

It is about your environment, and how well you fit in. Imagine being the child in the sandpit that takes the other child's toys. You are going to suffer for that.

Being selfish takes, while having self-hood gives. It is not about you, it is not about ME. It is not about US, or THEM, or THOSE. It's about Life and living it.

Your mother, on the other hand, wants to believe it is all about you. Why? She has invested her life in you. Her identity and self-worth are tied to her children. You are how she proves her worth to the world; therefore YOU become very important in her eyes. That's what mothers do. You can get a very skewed sense of your real value from this. Remember: life doesn't care what your mother thinks or believes.

Life is for living. If you are self-centered, if you think it is about YOU, life just passes you by.

Life is a river of NOW – it takes little interest in the person, and takes nothing personally: Life offers this river of being to all who wish to swim in this moment. But do you imagine that if you ignore this moment, and live in a world of suffering and despair, that life will stop? No, the river just keeps flowing.

When you take something that someone says personally, what you are doing is stepping out of the flow of life. When you think anything is about YOU, specifically, you are stepping from the flow of life.

Surrender Your Right to Take Offence

When you deeply understand it isn't about YOU, you surrender the right to take anything personally. Please remember: You cannot GIVE offense! Offense can only be TAKEN. The irony is that most people cannot even take a compliment, yet they can take offense!

So, someone slanders you with a racial slur? Well, so what? It's not about YOU, it is about THEIR issues.

Someone says you are too fat? OK, thanks for sharing. A person on Facebook accuses you of being a bigot. Well, I sincerely hope they find a resolution to the anger that is driving them.

Are you starting to understand? When you truly understand it is not about YOU, when you get that it is about life and living, then you begin to see what is driving everyone else. Surrender your right to take things personally, because it was never about you.

A perfect example is a friend in Holland. I called her just at the time her houseboat was being axed up by a jealous ex-boyfriend. I asked, "Have you rung the Police?" She said she hadn't and probably wouldn't.

Obviously, I asked why. She explained, *"He is driven by pain. He is destroying anything and everything he made for me. He thinks he will cure his pain by destroying any connection between us, so this is his way of surviving. It means it is finished now."*

I asked how she knew he would not come back, or worse stalk her, and cause greater problems.

She said, *"We only do that which we believe will help us to survive. All this is a way for his ego to survive rejection, and once his big statement is made, once he had 'proven' himself, then he will go away."*

She was 100% right. This is what happened. Now, I do NOT advocate letting abusers off the hook. Far from it, but as a result of his actions, and her calm response, everyone who knew the fellow tossed him out of his or her social circles. His boss fired him, no one would employ him in that town, and no one would talk to him. He was ostracized and had to move, buy a house elsewhere, and start a new life.

By seeing the obvious, by seeing things clearly, the problem my friend suffered was resolved quickly.

This woman had a deep understanding of human nature. The primary cause, the primary flame of that understanding, was that she knew it was not about her. The guy attacking her home? This wasn't about HER; it was about HIM and his wounded pride. It was not HER that caused the outbreak, but his insecurity.

She discovered the pearl of detachment in a world obsessed with self-interest and victim mentality, and because of this she is free. Pursuing the matter with the Police would have only activated a deeper level of insecurity and defensiveness in the man and he would have gone to another level of attack, believing he was protecting himself. It would have also meant having further dealings with him in court, etc.

She didn't need revenge, or a settlement, or further communication. She just wanted it finished.

It is not about us! When we practice being involved in life, rather than just ourselves, an amazing thing happens - We start "funning the day" - Many of our problems appear to fade away and we rediscover a childlike certainty of living in the moment. So tell me: What are we really doing when experiencing life and living it? We are living in the NOW. We are living in the moment - more importantly, we are living without concern about society's 'shoulds' or 'should nots'.

Our awareness now shifts from powerless to powerful. As we experience this moment, this NOW, unhappy thoughts and feeling fall away into our past.

All negatives evaporate when we step into the NOW. Conversely, the secret to know is that if you are experiencing a negative, you are not in the NOW.

How I learned Rule One

Let me assure you, I re-learn Rule One every day. All this started with heartbreak and an understanding about something that seemed the complete opposite. Many years ago I had a breakdown of sorts: My world fell to pieces, to the point that I was not able to eat or do anything. I spent six weeks living on just water.

It is not as hard as you might imagine – after the first five days, you no longer feel hungry. It was only when my muscles began to disappear that I reluctantly started having bread and fruit. I did this for another six weeks, while traveling about in the country.

I spent three months in the bush on almost nothing (It was a vision quest of sorts, but a blind one, if that makes any sense.) I wrote a book during that time, otherwise I might have thought it was all just a dream.

The up-shot of it all was that I had a Cosmic Realization about something that was strikingly dull. We like to imagine a Cosmic Realization is going to be all bells and whistles, the "Ah HA!" moment of Oprah. For me, no. It was so ordinary, so uninteresting, that it barely rated a mention in my Dream Journal.

I had gotten back to town after my three months of fasting and found myself at the local comedy club, at the public urinal. You know, the urinal, the place where men line up to surreptitiously inspect each other's dicks? They do, you know. Men pretend to be disinterested in the size and shape of the guy beside him, but they almost always glance over and check things out.

Well, I was shy. I always felt a little intimidated being on display and would usually duck into a toilet cubicle where I could close the door. But this day it struck me that all this shyness, it just didn't matter! The words came through clearly, "It's only me!"

And as this sank in, I saw the truth! *"It's only them, it's only me, it's only US."* We are all in it together. We are all here, now, and nowhere else. I felt a deep sense of relief because now I could use a public urinal.

But you would agree, this doesn't sound like much of a result for three months of starving yourself.

Even so, by accepting myself as I was, I was set free from what other people may or may not have thought. As time went by I began to understand – this was a big step upwards in my process of personal integration. As a consequence, a curious understanding began to germinate: I didn't need to solve anything! I could just accept myself and enjoy this moment.

I discovered I didn't need to PROCESS my problems - I could just LET THEM GO! And when I did, I was opened to a tremendous truth: *Nothing has to be rejected, nothing has to be cherished.* My problems were pieces on the chess board of my life, but there were no opponents! I was my enemy! By letting go of my attachment to my fears and concerns, I proved I was greater than they were. And here is the really weird part; by letting them go, I owned them. More to the point, they no longer owned ME. We could spend a book discussing this paradox, but we won't.

This understanding uncovered something else that surprised to me. *As I let go of my fears, I could see them more clearly.* I could see what they truly were, thus I was much better able to deal with them.

Even so, despite the fact that I knew it was 'only me', in my mind it was still all 'about' me. Sure, I was able to cope better and walk taller in my society. Certainly I was more confident and able to express myself more clearly in public: But it was still all about ME. I am not complaining, "It's only Me" was a major milestone, yet this was but the FIRST step towards freedom.

Now, when I met a pretty girl, instead of getting nervous I could say, *"It's just me, it's just her."* My acceptance meant we were able to communicate better.

But it was still all about what 'I' wanted out of the exchange. That's when it hit me! If she was interested, it was not about ME - it was because she wanted something for herself. "OH!" went a gong in my head. "It's all about self-interest!"

What this translates to is SO important: *What 'I' want is irrelevant to other people!* People only care about what THEY want. If the stars line up, you get lucky.

That's the real secret. That person you fancied, who you got all insecure about, trying to find the courage to go up to them? They are thinking exactly the same about someone else. Everyone is in the same boat UNTIL you understand that it is not about you.

Let's look at this - a mother with a newborn is more concerned about what her baby needs than what she wants. Two people deeply in love care only for what the other needs. A grandfather only cares that the grandchild grows up happy and content.

When the individual cares more for what is outside their immediate world, it is suddenly no longer about THEM! When we let go the monkey grip of self, and act in consideration of others, we set our heart and mind free.

Positive Indifference

The lasting cure for excessive self-interest, vanity by any other name, is to stop acting as if it is about you.

To do this effectively, we need to experience a state of positive indifference towards all things in our life.

Let me explain, it is important. Simple indifference to others while we remain focused on ourselves leads to cruelty. But a sincere indifference to our OWN opinions and beliefs, our own sense of importance, while retaining a deep and sincere interest in life – this is a POSITIVE state of indifference.

Humility may be the absence of vanity, but positive indifference is what starves it out of your life.

NB: When I say it is not about you, I am not saying YOU are unimportant - far from it. We are all important - what I am asking you to practice is a positive indifference to your notions of SELF importance. We are ALL important, and when respect this with an attitude of service and kindness to others, life starts to hum a happier tune.

Like a mother serving her new born, we no longer give ourselves priority. We start to wake into a state of consciousness where it is all about what we DO, how we SERVE, and who we HELP. And the paradox of Rule One: *For every piece of self importance we cast aside, a greater sense of self arises.* Each step on the rung of understanding that it is not about US leads us to a higher view, a clearer perspective of what we are.

When you accept that it is NOT about you, when you no longer desire anything to BE about you, it is amazing how much more you see. By not taking things personally, by not making everything about ourselves, we are set free to BE. It also stops the 'chatter' in the mind, the sense of whispers about others that holds the attention of the majority of people on this planet.

Your Inner Rat IS your perception, or more accurately, your ability to perceive. Why is this important? A clear view of your environment gives you an advantage in every area. You have all the lights on while everyone else is wandering about in the dark.

Let's reverse this, and see if it makes the message clearer. Most salesman focus intently on the person they are trying to sell something to. They ask leading questions in order to get people to talk about themselves. By making everything about YOU, the sales person encourages you to believe that you are worthy, interesting, accepted: everything you secretly fear you are not. In this way he/she gains your trust.

The salesperson wants you to believe it's all about YOU. Why? That is the best way to get your money.

The Effect of Rule One

Understanding and practicing Rule One has many curious effects. Apart from being better able to see what is obvious, because you are no longer looking through the clouded lens of self deception, you start to act differently: You release the monkey grip on the perception of self, and of others. You then allow a greater free flow of imagination, thought, and feeling.

Three things that might give you the inclination to make Rule One part of your daily practice:

First: *If you let someone talk about themselves for ten minutes, they will believe that you are their friend. When someone feels you are their friend, they not only believe more easily what you say, they are less likely to do you wrong.*

Second: *If you maintain an interest in things outside your self, you will not be easily introverted, therefore not easily controlled by external pressures.*

Third: *When you sincerely practice not placing yourself at the center of things, an odd thing happens. People want to bring you into their lives!*

I am not talking about getting fame or money, though this can happen. When it's not about YOU, the effect is you listen more to what others say - and people LIKE this. They will like YOU as a result.

Of course, now I go and spoil everything by publishing a book with my name on it. There it is, I have gone and put myself at the center of everything. That sort of proves I don't practice what I preach, hey? Well, tough. I am a RAT.

The Mystic Rat Says: *Truth comes in bubbles of thought, feeling and belief. But the paradox! If you cherish your truth, it stays in the bubble. You have to pop your hopes and dreams to realize them.*

Ergo: If you want to get to the secret inside, you may need to be a bit of a prick.

TWO:

Do Not Should in Your Own Nest

There are two saboteurs in your life. The basic saboteur is the SHOULD, the blind obedience to what we have been taught. The second is the first cousin of the SHOULD, the SORRY. Both are based on a nebulous fear of authority.

You SHOULD act this way, or that way, or do this thing, behave in that manner, etc. etc. And if you don't, "I am so SORRY I didn't follow the SHOULD!"

These twin notions form the rust that oxidizes your life and happiness. How do you get around it?

I had a girlfriend who had a curious habit: if anyone asked her to do something she did not want to do, she nodded with a strong agreement to their request, and said, "Yes, maybe!" She had no interest in what they offered; yet she voiced it in a way they could not take offence. She had the power of positive indifference.

This is the way to deal with external expectations of others and your internal fears of fitting in. There is no need to fight society, just sidestep it where you don't fit the picture. Learn a sense of, "Yes Maybe!"

People's expectations are not your greatest concern: YOU are the real concern. Are you shoulding in your own nest? Do we have invisible rules that instruct those around us how they 'should' behave? Are we allowing all to be who and what they want to be? The creeping in of the Should can be very subtle, and worse, it seems perfectly justified. Of course the dishes should be done, the lawn mowed, the house swept. They are essential for the smooth running of the house.

But HOW are you laying your expectations of behavior down? (On both yourself and others)

Rule Two is really the Law of Non-Interference. It can be very subtle but the principle is simple: When you break the boundary of self, you have SHOULDED on something. When you allow your self to be governed by the edicts of the external world rather than fixing your small part of it, then all your shoulds start to go plop on the floor behind you.

Shoulding is all over Facebook and social media now - It is a disease that has taken over society. Here's the thing to know: People who tell you what you 'should' do suffer a negative distortion of self-image. And if this affects you, it means you are lacking center.

All the collective shoulds of society have no power over a person who has found the still, certain point within. If you are strong within your own sense of self, the projected 'shoulds' from others are water off the duck's back.

To really get into this needs a discussion about the inner censor, which Jung spoke about. This is the gestalt of your social training and is a way the mind defines its position in the world.

Understand, when a person is telling others how they 'should' behave, it is often insecurity driving them. Their internal Censor is weak, and they are shoring up their self-esteem by getting others to agree to their invisible rules.

Your CENSOR is important: It is the gestalt of your social training and upbringing. It is the inner set of rights and wrongs that define your actions and command you to act in set ways. When this is weak, you "Should" on others to force them into agreement with you. (or your beliefs) By doing so you feel stronger and more in control.

Here is the thing: *When we pull back from our opinions and notions of what SHOULD be, we soon realize an extraordinary thing: Only people suffering a lack of self-respect will insist on you doing what you 'should'. Ergo: People who use authority to control others lack a deep sense of self-worth.*

Conversely, those who refuse to 'should' on others have a strong self-image.

This is where it gets complicated

We all share a social upbringing that has programed us to act in particular ways. But by not understanding you are running on a program, you are shoulding on yourself. How so? The program you were raised with is a list of shoulds. By not consciously stopping this, the natural result is to should on things. It gets worse.

People have an ingrained belief that, if their shoulds are stronger than other people's shoulds, then they are in some way the winner. History is littered with despots and cruel plantation owners, all who firmly believed they were winning. They wield the power of the SHOULD, and they control the destiny of others, therefore they are powerful. But really, they are controlled by their own internal state of SHOULD.

We all want to be cause, but often we are in the effect of others. EG: The boss can SHOULD on you, and you can do little about it, because you might be fired if you object. So what do you do? Gossip about how bad he is? Bitch to workmates that he 'should not' act like this towards you?

The should is insidious. It creeps into everything.

Of course, YOU are not a despot. You may have a strong center, you may be strong in your will and fierce in your determination, but you have principles and do not try and rope others in on your personal state of should. You deserve a MEDAL - Yet, here you are, still SHOULDING on yourself. You are still doing what you believe you 'should'.

The "should" disease is all pervasive. It has taken over the Western World like a mold that eats into its vital organs. What's more, this is not going to change quickly. The SHOULD is a chronic condition at the heart of Western Society and it will take decades, possibly generations, to pass. But you can stop shoulding on yourself. You can do this right now!

Why 'should' you? To control your inner dialogue. Every time you employ a 'should' to control your personal behavior, you are entering into an internal dialogue. THIS snips you from the flow of life. THIS makes you a slave to your pre-installed program.

The Internal Dialogue

This is the Censor at work, the voice inside that tells you what you should do. This voice is not your conscious self, it speaks from the subconscious.

It is a program, installed by parents and peers and it offers a set of instruction of what you 'should' do.

How do we clearly define the inner voice of your highest truth from the echo of shoulds inside us? First, we pause the action of SHOULD in our life.

I will not on about the physiological basis of the SHOULD, coming from the Medulla Oblongata, the basis of the program for breath and other autonomic responses in the body. It is not just a psychological whispering, there is a physical neurological pattern lodged in the back of the brain – It takes time and effort to weed out the crop of shoulds in our life – but when we do, we receive the gift of true freedom.

Freedom means we live moment to moment. Yes, we plan, organize, focus on goals, etc. We do not stop the process of doing what we MUST, we pause our 'should. We stop acting on the basis of SHOULD.

The ability to stop shoulding on our self opens up Rule THREE, "Keep one eye open". This is dependant on Rule Two. If you are listening to a 'should' you are looking at instructions from the past, which cuts you from NOW. This makes you blind to the obvious, therefore you fail Rule Three.

Rule Two: Stop SHOULDING in your own nest.

Stop SHOULDING on Yourself! But how? It is both more difficult, and far easier, than you might imagine.

To refute the habit of should, we need to understand a simple truth: *There is not a single SHOULD in your head that is YOURS.* No baby is born with a SHOULD in their heart or mind. ALL notions of 'Should' are IMPLANTS. It's not that they are "bad", they are just control measures put in place by parents and society in order to keep things organized.

Imagine what a mess it would be if people did whatever they would, instead of what they should? The wheels of commerce would slow, the schools would empty, and the entire economy would falter and degenerate back to the Stone Age.

What is the inheritance you offer your children? More Shoulds? Or something better?

Please understand: The structure of our society, our commerce, our financial services – they are all wrapped around 'shoulds'.

SHOULDS are a necessary part of existence. They are the ORDER CREATORS in our social framework.

Tell a titan of industry or a bureaucrat that his or her shoulds are wrong and it is a slap in their face – you would be laughed at, or worse, imprisoned for your dangerous rhetoric.

I have had friends send to jail for daring to upset the should cart. One friend foolishly declared that, as the free passage of traffic on the Kings Road was a Tort, it had greater weight than State legislature.

He argued a Roman Tort: that, as a person driving had the right to travel the road, the police only had the right to pull him over and do breathalyzer tests if he appeared to be driving erratically. He was entirely correct in his assessment of the law, yet is currently contemplating his rightness behind bars.

This is why all good Rats keep their OWN house in order, and do not seek to correct the rights or wrongs of others, or society – as soon as you start down that road, you are shoulding on the shoulders of society.

Let's be clear: If you can keep yourself in order, you do not need a 'should' to create order. This is obvious. But others can find your apparent disregard for their shoulds very annoying. It is a bit of a balancing act, but I can tell you a secret: A person who speaks well, dresses well, whose house is in order, and whose bills are paid is left alone by authority. The trick to rising above the tide of should in our lives is to find a state of order within ourselves. WANT to have a tidy room, not tidy because you 'should'. WANT to have clean dishes, not clean them because you 'should'.

If you get nothing else from this whole book, get this: *Stop SHOULDING on yourself.* This stupid act of self-terrorism separates you from the Book of Life.

Shoulding on yourself keeps you imprisoned in other people's beliefs and it makes you a puppet on a string controlled by anyone who cares to tug your beliefs.

SHOULDS are everywhere, in everything, and on everyone's shoulders - like the proverbial Monkey on the Back. They are hateful monsters, yet as a society we need them.

Imagine a world without shoulds? *"Imagine there's no shoulding, it's easy if you try!"* Seriously, imagine people sitting out in the sun enjoying their days rather than sitting in air-conditioned boxes slaving over useless paperwork. Imagine doing what fulfils you rather than what makes money for the boss! Can you see how society would collapse? It would ruin everything.

It's a shocking thought, one that must be rejected out of hand.

Shoulds are cornerstones in the psychic framework of society. Shoulds are the main tool of controllers.

They are a means to contain the wild beast, the rapist, the thief, and the murderer inside us. And that is fair enough: Society had to evolve, and it evolved through negative control measures such as the SHOULD.

Religions, of course, are the single greatest source of Should and Should Not. But we also find them running through families, peer groups, and work places.

The Flow of SHOULDS from the outer world into your brain is fully established and you will have a huge battle to fully remove them. In fact, you will never get rid of them all, they are too ingrained. So, what is the cure? The first step is an important one – it is to remove the word SORRY from your vocabulary.

Exterminate Your Sorry!

Remove the word 'Sorry' from your vocabulary.

This is easier to say than do. Surely, if you do someone wrong, apologize, and do so earnestly: It is part of our social contract that we do not intimidate or hurt others. But avoid using the SORRY word.

Why? Using it means almost the opposite. Just as your RAT is your Reality Attention Trigger, the word 'sorry' is the worlds strongest PUP. A PUP is a Personal Un-integration Point.

Technically Un-Integration is not really a word, but non-integration implies you are NOT connected, whereas Un-Integration tells us that we are, but not properly - so I use it. Un-Integration best explains the effect of SORRY on your Psyche. SORRY is used as an apology for living. It keeps you in pieces, it stops you collecting yourself and standing up straight to face the world Eye to Eye.

Saint Paul said: "At first, through the Glass Darkly, and then Face to Face".

If you want to get face to face with life, you must get through the 'Sorry Barrier'. Apologizing for your existence is a form of demeaning yourself, and it clouds your view. It is a way of bowing down and worshipping the false idol of the Should God and it

ALSO puts you squarely into the concept that you are the center of things.

Think! If it is not about you, why are 'you' apologizing? But if it IS about you, if you have done someone wrong, apologize sincerely, then pick up and dust off. The real truth is that the word 'Sorry' is rarely used as a recognition you are at fault, and far more as an avoidance of responsibility.

You bump into someone and say, "Sorry." But it means nothing – you are not actually sorry, it's just a word. We all bump into things, it is not something to be sorry for – quite the opposite, it is something to celebrate! It means you are alive. When you say your unthinking, "sorry", you blindly apologize for your existence - you cover yourself in a shower of should.

Bad, very bad.

"At first, through the glass darkly, and then - Face to Face!" Saint Paul is talking about the discovery of Soul, the perpetual Spark, the great knowing within. If you want to connect with this, it requires REMOVING the concept of SORRY from your brain. Let me stress - We are not refuting the genuine apology. We refute the avoidance of this by using a term such as 'sorry'.

We are speaking about removing the pattern of apologizing for your life. Removing this attitude brings us into a stronger sense of NOW. Saint Paul is alluding to the importance of meeting your personal divinity in the here and now, discovering your Soul, finding your beingness. The process to get to this place of clarity is "through the Glass Darkly" - Why is the glass dark? I kind of doubt he is meaning God wears Raybans. Is it because the light is obscured by your SHOULDS?

One thing I know: Only when we get this notion of vague personal wrongness sorted can we begin to understand, "Face to Face".

SORRY is such a dreadful word. It is a MAGNET for every SHOULD in the Universe to come calling on you. Even when you apologize to yourself or another, in terms of, "I should not have done that!" you are still

SHOULDING on yourself. However, when you say, "That was poor judgment on my part. I apologize!" you are not shoulding, you are affirming.

This gives opportunity for dialogue and a far more meaningful direction. You are AFFIRMING your right to life even as you admit a mistake. Surely, we must apologize to any and all we may have done wrong to, but to survive this world of 'should' we must do so with the attitude of making it RIGHT, rather than bathing in a worry of wrongness.

A Rat in a Restaurant

AVOID the word Sorry and you will start to see the difference in your life. As a small example: I ran a restaurant. (Yes, someone put a RAT in charge of the restaurant, can you believe?) One night a woman was served a chicken pastry meal when she had ordered a vegetarian one. No problem - just let the staff know and you get the proper meal.

Obviously, she complained and you always do your best to improve the clients dining experience. However, when I came over I saw that she had eaten almost all of her chicken and was now squawking about how it had poisoned her. I simply stopped, looked closely at the lack of remains on her plate, and raised one eyebrow.

You must understand how POWERFUL a raised eyebrow is, especially when combined with a lack of apology. It says so much without saying anything at all. It says you doubt everything the person is saying because you can see the OBVIOUS. The person KNOWS they are angling for a freebie, or trying to get some case up to sue you, or whatever. But by saying nothing and just observing the obvious, you do more damage to their aggression than anything else.

The legal Term is "Res Ipsa Loquitur". It means, "The thing speaks for itself". In other words, it is recognizing that which is obvious through manner or word.

Here I will share with you the secret on how to apply this in order to gain the greatest effect. If you want your Inner Rat to grow, if you wish to survive better in this world, then do the simplest of things: Nothing! Just STOP and WAIT. The PAUSE can be POWERFUL. Just WAIT a moment before proceeding.

I raised an eyebrow, took a deep breath, looked at the woman for a moment, then said, "I can truly see how terrible this must be for you. How can I help solve this problem for you? What can I give you that will lessen this blow?"

The woman got her dander up, and started decrying:

1. she might DIE from this meat,

2. she had not eaten meat for nineteen years,

3. and how shocking it was that this could happen!

So I nodded in agreement with everything she said and, of course. I noted how she made this all about her, so I also made sure the offending item remained on her table. Further, I made not a single comment on the fact that it was mostly eaten. I just waited for her to say what she actually wanted. She never did.

"Res Ipsa Loquitur" was what I kept in mind.

I simply concurred with all she had said. "I completely agree with you, Madam. What can I DO to help solve this for you? Free Dessert? A Port? What can I offer you?" I then explained how we had a new chef and that the pastry for the vegetable dish had a 'V' on it that can look like a 'C' – for Chicken. An honest mistake, not an assassination attempt.

Whatever I said, I refused absolutely to say SORRY. I was reasoned, calm and clear and offered to help in any way I could. As a result, a curious thing happened.

Her boyfriend was embarrassed and began to take MY side. He started arguing that it was not unreasonable of me to try and offer what I could to help her. He stopped short of saying "Hey, you ate most of the chicken before you realized it was meat?" but we ALL knew this was the baseline fact.

Res Ipsa Loquitur!

So what does the woman do? She turns ALL her venom on the boyfriend, and THEN she becomes sweet as apple pie to me. Ah Ha! I have discovered a CAT. This woman had a CAT running her. (Controller And Terrorist) The restaurant broke a 'should', and as a CAT she wanted people to grovel and apologize. She was a control freak, and wanted to place myself in a position of WRONGNESS! Why?

It is very simple: it makes her feel important.

Paradoxically, this is what SHOULDING on ourselves does: It makes us feel important. We are in charge, we are telling ourselves what we SHOULD do!

The truth is: Shoulding on ourselves places us in a position UNDER the Powers that Be – A place where you become CONTROLLABLE by the Negative Energies that rule this planet. The CAT in the woman wanted blood. When she could not get it from me, she turned on the weakest point close to her, her boyfriend. (I was guessing, soon to be ex-boyfriend.)

THEN she started purring around MY leg, making pretty eyes, acting sweet and nice. I suspected I was intended as her next victim - I mean - lover. But CATS do not have lovers: they have objects of lust. They are vicious, emotionally dangerous, and if you are foolish enough to marry one, they will treat you like dirt – They desire to own you, emotionally, mentally and financially. Once owned, you become a chattel.

However, it is easy to negotiate with most of the controllers we meet by simply REMOVING the concept of 'sorry' from our psyche. They will not only respect you for it, they will then want to buddy up.

Does this surprise you? I can see no reason why it might - CATs are vain and lonely creatures that need a lap. This time she came up against a Rat who was awake to her game, so she lost that round.

This story gives us an opportunity to see how powerful avoiding 'sorry' can be. Here is the thing to grasp, by not giving an automated response, a reflex 'sorry', we create space for dialogue. We create space and allow a greater reality into our passing moments.

Let's look at the very basic Anti-Rat mistakes the woman made:

1. She acted as if it was all about her

2. She tried to should on others

Are you getting the bigger picture here? When you apply these first two Rat Rules, you will avoid coming under the control of authoritarians and controllers.

Controllers love to make you WRONG. In the restaurant, because I did not use a self-depreciating 'sorry' attitude, the woman gained no leverage to own the situation with her shoulds.

She tried to lay blame and fault on the basis that someone broke the rules! But there were no rules broken, no insult intended, it was a simple mistake by a new chef. All her efforts to make others look small and guilty reversed on herself, and rightly so.

Opposite to the above, I was at a cinema one evening and a pretty young thing accidentally stood on my toe. She automatically said, "Sorry!"

I laughed and replied, "No, Please - Do it again. I love it when pretty girls step on my toes."

She looked up, puzzled. Then she smiled, saying, *"Yeah, I guess it is like apologizing for Life, hey?"*

And THAT, dear reader, is the whole sorry business in a nutshell.

Remember this: *A Should is a Could that failed to grow past being a Would.* People who 'should' on others are controllers, and they generally are this way because they do not love their own life. Critics are all mostly 'Shoulders' and, as a point of observation, many of the really negative critics are significant failures in the very profession they now professionally critique.

The Mystic Rat Says: *Find the "why" or the motivation in any given situation and you can iron out just about any problem. Find the "why" and you have discovered your personal (wait for it) ... Iron-y*

Forget turning Lead into Gold! What is more important is to steel the spine, see the obvious, and be unafraid to ask the hard questions.

How about the Covid scare? A vast movement of SHOULD was put out, to require you to wear masks, not socialize, and cower in fear. Everywhere was pumping out the message of what you SHOULD do.

What will the long-term affect of all this "Shoulding" be? Will we see a new race of people, more aware and alert as to how fear is used to control the populace? We just might.

THREE:

Keep One Eye Open

The Third Rule is based on the ancient Eye of Horus: The All-Seeing Eye. This is spatial awareness personified. *Keep One Eye Open* means much more than being aware of your surroundings, it also means being conscious of your beingness. This aids your SURVIVAL. Keeping one eye open tells your consciousness to stay alert and to be careful, which is both:

1. *Full of Care, and*
2. *Cautious.*

Your RAT sniffs both opportunity and danger. It never sleeps unless you ignore it, so the Third Rule is a reminder to keep your RAT awake. This means feeding it. If you want to keep your sentry dog alert, you have to feed it – but here I may surprise you - you feed it with doubt. Forget positive mental attitude, your RAT eats your doubt and turns it into awareness.

The song went: *The night has a thousand eyes.* This implies everyone is watching you, yes? Sounds like a deep paranoia at work, yet this is true. Your phone tracks you. Facebook permeates every corner. The net holds thousands of opinions and beliefs that circulate around us every day via media, friends, and social groups. People are full of faulty judgment and poor logic. They hold up their 'shoulds' of half-truths and semi-lies, all based on past programming - A world that is all "I", "me" and "mine" - So, how do we fight through all this and keep our own house in order?

We keep one eye open. We seek to give ourselves a Triple "A" rating - *Awake, Alive, and Aware.*

AWAKE: If external influences bring us to the point where we are no longer able to respond to life, we are disobeying Rule Three. We must remain awake to be able to respond to our environment. Being drunk to the point of oblivion or taking drugs to the point of forgetfulness is breaking Rule Three. It will cost you.

It is really about responsibility - The ability to respond is to be able change course when danger makes you vulnerable. Look at the Titanic, stiff, unwavering opinion made the Captain blind to the obvious. Likewise, using drugs or booze to avoid pain can make you blind to the present moment.

But far worse, you are rejecting life. The drug addict or drunk is sending a message to life that they are not happy where they are. It is like chanting a prayer for things to go wrong. Life ALWAYS listens, and responds to the message you send it. Accordingly, Life will respond to your wish! It will bring you situations of difficulty and stress, which you secretly prayed for.

Every choice we make to be unaware of our surroundings is a prayer to life for things to go wrong.

Here is a little secret: Doing what you "should" is a choice to be unaware of your options. Doing what is 'expected' dries up your chance for fun. It is the weight of Shoulds, the pressure of expectation, and the lack of faith in yourself that generally drives the negative wheels in your clock.

Remember, these are CHOICES you are making – Whether unconscious or otherwise, the choice to listen to the inner whispers takes you away from NOW.

Indulgence equals Pain

The Ancient Greeks wrote about this on the Temple of Apollo in Delphi. We all know the right hand side, which is inscribed with the famous "Know Thyself". But lesser known one on the left hand side, says, "Nothing too much".

The Temple of Apollo at Delphi also has inscribed, "Make a pledge and destruction is near" - but we will leave that one for now.

You may have thought that living the life of the RAT meant living a life of indulgence - Far from it, dear reader. RATS are careful creatures. They obey the rule, "Nothing Too Much". They are frugal creatures that lives for the family.

Animals stay awake to their environment, because natural selection is a killer. While it is true, cows will eat magic mushrooms, parrots will get drunk on fermented nectar, but this is a random event, an occasional treat.

Keeping One Eye Open means to remain aware of the moment. Just as the sailor on the ocean can feel the current shifting under his feet, the awake soul feels the winds of change and adjusts their sails BEFORE the gale arrives to capsize the boat. We do NOT live in a harmonious, peaceful world. This is a World of War, a place of enormous greed with a deep lack of respect for others. We MUST keep our awareness; we MUST keep our wits about us if we are to survive.

Sentries

Life IS a war, so what does an army do to ensure survival? It keeps one eye open! It places sentries on watch. We would do well to copy this, but in a different way. We look for 'Sentries' that are specific markers. Look to nature, such as the behavior of ants. If ants get overly active for no apparent reason this is a clue there is a change in climate happening around you. Usually it means rain or a storm is coming.

Immediately prior to the huge Tsunami that killed 200,000 people in Indonesia and surrounding areas, ALL the native animals on the island of Aceh (the worst hit island) moved to higher ground. Did any of the locals pay attention?

No, and they drowned as a result. They did not keep one eye open.

We will get to this more in Ratology Two, but in summary, Life has a SOUND. You can hear it and, when a change is about to occur, a signal is sent that nature hears. You can hear it as well, if you listen. (Doctors will call it Tinnitus) But most sentries are far more obvious. We know when seasons are changing by the turning of leaves on the trees, and the shortening or lengthening of days.

But there are less subtle signs. Native Americans know when the salmon will arrive because BEARS start acting in specific ways. They are SENTRIES that tell you when change is to come. Only experience and wisdom will teach you this truth, but suffice to say, nature is attuned to the FREQUENCY of life.

SO! Learn to LISTEN to life around you and much trouble can be avoided. How do we listen to Life? Well, this is a problem for people who are either locked in mind stuff, stoned on drugs, or spinning out with emotional benders. But if you can get off the wheel of your circumstances and get closer to the NOW you will hear it. And when you hear it, you will realize you have been listening to Life ... well... all your Life!

It is a very real thing, called by many names over millennia. *"In the beginning there was the Word,"* is one we all know. Life is always bringing us 'the word' but are we listening?

You may find this funny, but often when I have a big hand in poker, and someone hits me with a big bet, I will stop and listen to the songs the cards are singing.

If it seems to me that I have less harmony in my cards, I fold them. I let it go and allow life to keep telling me what it will.

It's all about awareness, setting up sentry posts, and remaining attuned to the natural currents. We all have a better chance when we are forewarned. Keeping one eye open means you are placing perception to the forefront of your thoughts. It means you WANT to see the obvious. It is practicing mindfulness but it is also an expectation of discovering the unexpected. It cultivates an attitude that nothing is too much, that you can cope with whatever comes, and survive.

This is what the Eye of Horus will bring you.

National Geographic Article

https://tinyurl.com/3r2n3e2m

Jan 4 2005: National Geographic published an article (above) about how animals on the island of Aceh seemed to 'know' a tidal wave was coming.

This is NORMAL behavior, echoed in thousands of eye witness accounts over the centuries.

The REAL question to ask it, why did the locals not notice it? Nature has its sentries, it gives plenty of warning of impending events. We can be sure that before Pompeii was destroyed, they would have been given many signals.

Not paying attention to the messages we are sent, by natures sentries in particular, can have fatal results.

FOUR:
Ask No Favors
(Neither a beggar nor borrower be)

In no society is stagnation an option. People need progress, they need the sense they are going somewhere. In early society, this was all about barter, exchanging what you have for what you need. This meant that the best negotiators had the best life. Rule Four 'sounds' like it is about being totally independent, and it is, but at its core it is all about negotiation – how to get the things we need without incurring drama or karma.

The Jewish proverb, "Credit for necessities - Cash for luxuries," is the key. I am NOT saying do not use the banks. If you have a family and need to get the kids to school, etc. you NEED a stable house. This is a necessity and requires a mortgage.

The reason for Rule Four is stress. Maybe you get approved for the mortgage on a house, but then you see one with a Jacuzzi, a marble kitchen, five bedrooms, etc. – things that inflate the mortgage to stress levels.

Of course, the true Rat finds the bargains at a great price. The Merchant Rule states that if you can move something on for more than you paid, this is an investment, not a cost. Common sense applies.

The PROBLEM is that this modern age of excess drives us to get MORE. The general concept is driven by a MEME that comes from Victorian England: *The industrious soul is always forging ahead.* It is 'kind of' true - But many enslave themselves to their future dreams, and lose the NOW. There is nothing to prove. Our only duty is to come to each moment with clarity.

This means not complicating our life with unnecessary obligations or obfuscations.

To meet obligations we DO have to do the odd job that is not pleasing. We DO have to buckle down and move through times that are not fun. But we do NOT have to become a cog in the machinery of commerce. Specifically, we must never put ourselves into the position of being a beggar – how so? Why?

We avoid becoming a slave to the machine by simply taking responsibility for our personal situation. There are no victims, only circumstances we are not yet in charge of. There are difficult positions we get into, but every problem has a solution, we just have to find it. As to WHY we do not put ourselves in the position of a beggar, it is all about freedom and clarity.

In every scenario of our life, we must meet our circumstances and CHOOSE one of three actions.

- Do we agree with it?
- Do we change it? Or
- Do we leave it?

Inside the choice we make, there is the path that leads us through it – This path has three options.

- *Negative: We can believe we are not strong enough to do it ourselves.*
- *Positive: We can rely solely on our personal prowess and ability.*
- *Or the Balanced Path: We can call on life to help us out.*

Rule Four is not just about borrowing or lending – It is about creating harmony in the moment and developing a connection with life.

Harmony and freedom are ESSENTIAL. For things are to work out well for us, these are the energies that bring LIFE FORCE to bear in our lives. Without a natural life force on our side, it is a battle we can't win on our own. So, we will need favors from others to help us survive. Asking a bank or worse, a relative, for a loan to pay bills is never a good place to be. But in this and in ALL situations, we must use the power of NEGOTIATION to bring the best outcome to our side.

Negotiation: Fair Trade is No Mans Loss

Here is the rub: While we must lean on life for assistance, we still need to connect with others. We need to communicate, bargain, trade, and *negotiate* - And this is where Rule Four applies - The secret of all successful negotiation is to come to the table with a sense of authority and strength. Confident calculation and a clear perception of the benefits we are offering is what tilts things in our favor. All successful negotiation is based on one constant: That which is good for all is good for each.

So how do you make things better for yourself? *The trick for getting the best outcome is to approach all our dealings with others with the sense that we already possess everything we need, that what we are ask for is simply a reasonable addition to what already exists.*

In other words: We do not approach things as a beggar, asking for favors.

The Law of Nature is: *Much gathers more, less gathers loss*. When we have an attitude of 'LOTS' life tends to give us 'More'. Even when we lose a few rounds, this attitude keeps the energy of success flowing, and THIS is far more effective than positive thinking in generating best possible outcomes. Even better: Generate a sense of generosity in all your dealings: *I have LOTS and I am willing to share!*

Done well, you never need to ask favors because you truly believe you do not need them. You DO ask for a deal, however.

Rule Four is very much about finding a point of balance between your needs and those of your community. *Ask No Favors:* Be self-contained to the greatest possible degree and offer fair trade for what you need. Be a good citizen and do not rely on others to support your lifestyle. It is pretty simple stuff. The qualifier is where it gets interesting. Do you remember the phrase: *"Neither a Beggar nor Borrower be"*? This comes from Shakespeare's 'Hamlet', and is an old axiom about not incurring debt.

Have you considered this implies not to be a LENDER, as well? If borrowing and begging is bad, then the Lender is an essential part of the equation, yes? This phrase (and Rule Four in general) really means: *Do not to bind yourself to others.*

This statement comes with a qualifier. Being married is a binding contract. You are bound to that person - Rule Four does not mean living independent of everyone, or having no personal relationships, etc. Rule Four relates to the subtle chains that lie IN BETWEEN the contracts we enter into in this life.

I woke one day with an extraordinary revelation. I had spent the night looking at fine wires – they tied the universe together. These 'wires' represented the natural forces, gravity, light, etc.

But when I woke I saw different sorts of wires, I saw the binding agreements that people make. Contracts, both emotional and mental, that people had taken out between each other. I saw very clearly how so many people are living in co-dependant relationships and effectively tied up and bound by a long series of what were quite unbeneficial agreements.

Then it went "click"! Most people are in relationships where they are borrowing or lending energy with their mate and/or associates. They are stitching themselves up with Wires of Convention,

Memes of Should, and Lines of Expectations – So much tying down, and to what benefit? Mostly, it is for convenience. And when it becomes inconvenient, snip things with a divorce. Instead of finding resolution, fair trade in other words, people rebel against the control lines they feel ensnared in.

So what exactly am I talking about? What are these control lines?

Under the surface of normal communication are thousands of tiny contracts between people. These strings that bind become the bars of our prison – bars created by us! It is all a CONTRACT – you do this, and I will do that. We all have done this to some degree. Often this is an unwritten contract, but a binding one, regardless of the lack of ink or signatures. We rarely read the fine print of the emotional and mental agreements we enter into. But, if you ask the right questions, you can snap out of it.

Quite by chance, if you believe in chance, soon after the dream of wires I was down at Byron Bay. Something said to go into a hippie shop that had opened. Now, while I had no need for bongs or cheese cloth shirts, I listened, and obeyed the inner nudge. Inside, I was surprised to meet Gerry, a fellow I knew who ran a large business supplying health bars to shops nationwide. What was he doing here?

We got talking, and it turned out he had been cheated out of his business, a multi-million dollar enterprise. He had lost his wife, his house, and his income. So, he went to the religion he had been a faithful member of for many years and asked if he could build a small house on the riverfront land he had GIVEN them some years earlier. It was an acreage property and he asked if he might go into a quiet corner, stressing he would be completely out of the way.

Remember, Gerry had GIVEN them the river front property, no strings, just gave it away. Well, they told him to piss off. Well, they told him to piss off.

Losing My Religion

So, on top of the wife, kids, the business, and his house, Gerry also lost his religion. You might think he had a right to be bitter, to criticize, to denigrate the ungrateful wretches - he did none of this.

He found this shop for rent that had accommodation out back and it was cheap. So he rented it and started a shop. It was a hit! The place was going gangbusters!

What impressed me most was how Gerry was genuinely happy, despite his adversity. *"I am glad they wouldn't let me build a house on the property I gave them,"* he said. *"Now my eyes are opened, I see things as they really are. Yes, I was cheated by scumbags, I lost everything, but all it means is that everything that TIED ME DOWN is now GONE! I am now truly free, for the first time in my life."*

Gerry had been forcibly woken up out of his prison, but he HAD woken up. Many years later, life was to deliver myself the exact same message - remembering Gerry's smiling face helped me deal with the loss.

The message is very simple, we cannot rely on another to supply our happiness. We get married thinking this will make us happy. We buy a new house, a new car, believing this will make us happy. We get into all sorts of social and financial contracts, thinking this will bring us happiness.

There is nothing WRONG with this. In truth, all the strings and attachments we wrap around ourselves, they form the cocoon that allows us to go through the internal change that, eventually, brings us to freedom.

But in finding this point of freedom, we discover our greatest curse are those little beliefs and agreements that now tie us down. Caterpillars turn to butterflies, but only if they can escape their cocoon.

We bind ourselves to others through deeds, beliefs, identifications, and considerations. If we hold the belief of being greater or lesser than another, if we think our religion is more important than we are, if we compare our lives with others: All this means is that we are tying ourselves into invisible contracts.

SO! How do we make contracts that DO NOT bind us? It is the principle of Fair Trade. An old Yorkshire saying goes: *"Fair Trade is no man's loss!"*

Rule Three is more than a fair exchange of money, energy, or whatever does not bind you with invisible strings. There are also gifts from life, like oxygen, water, and three dimensions. (Ever thought to be grateful for that third dimension?) Where is the trade?

Life gives without a stipulating a return and by accepting its gift we are not bound to anything.

Yet this IS a contract: We breathe in oxygen and give back CO_2 to the plants that in return give us oxygen.

The simple way to ensure our actions in life remain mutually beneficial. Create a BENEFIT.

If we wish to grow, discover love, and create a better life, we have to do more than eat, breath, piss, and crap. We need to show people a BENEFIT. As we enter into agreements with those around us, with work, with general living, show that your presence is a BENEFIT. This ensures freedom and harmony.

Social contracts are part of human existence, so how can we have these yet not be bound by them? The first step is *"Fair Trade is No Man's Loss"*. The second is to show a benefit. The third is what truly matters – the thing that sets *us* free: *Do without thought of reward.*

Do Without Thought of Reward

While all this "RAT" stuff sounds selfish, it isn't. Quite the opposite – the way to keep your RAT wide-awake is with generosity. Altruism, acts of simple kindness, are not just food for the RAT – they also leave us free of entanglement. Altruism is pure OUTFLOW – its actions contain no internalizing energy to invert you. You can be working for the boss, doing your job, but an altruistic agreement does not have a slave/master option.

You simply do your best, without thought of reward, because that is what you WANT to do.

True altruism, however, is exceedingly rare. Most 'gifts' from others are Trojan Horses. This is the harsh reality of life. But if you are doing without thought of reward, that no longer bothers you. On a personal level, when we expect no favors from others, nor grant favors on the basis of GETTING something, we find a better point of balance. We are also better able to spot the ties that bind.

It is good to help others, but is there an attitude of gaining favor because of your kindness? This removes the 'actual' kindness from the equation, yes? This is where we miss the boat. Even when you believe you are being kind and wonderful, if, under the surface, there is a wish to gain as a result of your actions you are setting yourself up as a lender, not a giver.

Which is fine, as long as you know it.

If you know the truth, everything is fine. And the truth is: *Playing the White Knight creates a Debt!* When you covertly or overtly want something in return for your help you have LENT another your good will and kindness. And what did you trade for?

You may need a sense of importance, you may be looking for a sense of worthiness, or perhaps you just want someone indebted to you. You have to know yourself in order to know your true motivations and as so few of us know ourselves, the simple guideline is this: Sure, help someone if they need it and you can afford it, but GIVE them this help, do not LEND it.

By the same token, if someone wants to GIVE you help and assistance (Like I am offering with this book) feel free to accept it. Just remember fair trade: Don't buy into an invisible agreement where we OWE or are OWED. The Beggar and Borrower and Lender enter into a Karmic Agreement, but the GIVER is free. I give this information freely. You owe me nothing unless you downloaded a pirated copy of this book.

Identifying the Beggar/Borrower

It is easy to say, "do not a beggar or borrower be" but recognizing this situation is often not so simple. We see the beggar on the street - If I give them money do I create a lender - beggar relationship?

Giving money to a person who asks for it IS a contract, but for what? It depends on HOW it is given. How and why you interact establishes the karma, or pattern. When I give a person in the street a few coins it is because they asked for help. It is a simple exchange, you need some money, I have some spare. It is a gift and part of a larger wheel than either of us.

Yet if I give money thinking, "There but for the grace of God go I!" this is a very different story. I have invested more than spare change; I have put into this exchange a whole raft of belief. It is the arrogance of the statement that binds you. You have put yourself above the beggar. Under the pretence of charity you are saying you are superior.

Perhaps I give money with strings attached, "You have to spend this on food, not on booze." etc. This is shoulding on the person.

Maybe I give money because I need to look good to others in the street? Or because I am afraid they have a knife? So many reasons other than, "They look as if they need a few coins."

WHY we enter into these relationships is where the karma is set up. If I act out of pure charity, there is no complication – I am not fishing for any sort of return. That said, there are many tricks people use to fish US.

One of the common ones is a person presenting you with a bill that is unfair or which is not yours. Let's say a person staying at your house buys a hose for the backyard – They spend $39 at the hardware, then they give you the receipt saying you owe them the money.

No, you don't. They bought the hose, it does not matter what the reason was, or whom it was for. When they leave, they have the right to take the hose with them. You may object, saying it was not your decision to buy it, and they may respond with, "Well you can't use my hose then!" They are begging your favor!

We all know how petty people can be. The correct response is to ask them to either share the hose, or to remove it from the common area. Defining fine points like this are necessary for harmony. Clearly denoted boundaries are important.

You may offer a solution, offer to pay for half the hose, but what happens when the fellow leaves? Far better to have clear, easy to determine boundaries. Good fences make good neighbors, and all that.

Far less certain are interpersonal contracts. A person may have sexual relations with another, and expect certain 'credits' in return. This is different, as something has been shared. A whole set of conditions may emerge for what was offered or what you took.

Clearly, I am not talking about a love relationship, where both parties freely give. More confusing is where you THINK it is a love relationship, but for the other person it was merely an exchange.

Most people have relation-shops. I do this, you do that, so we agree to continue. Breaking the 'rules' has consequences and resolving them is a matter of barter. This is a beggar, or need, relationship. You need this, they offer that. They want that, you give them this. Etc. Most beggar relationships are covert and it is important to be able to recognize them as and when they arise.

Some examples:

Implied Guilt: The person presents you with a cost or a charge, saying this is fair – despite the fact you never made any agreement with them in regards the matter. (The hose story above)

Implied Debt: A person does a service, or a favor, and expects repayment. Or worse, constantly reminds you of all they have done for you!

The "Put Me" Trap: A person places things into your personal world as a way of claiming it. They may present them as gifts, but they 'put' a thing in your personal space to make a claim of ownership.

They want to put themselves into your life, and are using gifts and tokens to get a foot in the door. This 'put' can be sexual favors or physical objects. They are things that come with covert expectations.

The "you said!" trap: A person claims, "You said this!" when you object to some action or interference. This is hard to deal with, unless you have a diary of every little thing you agreed to.

The "Logical Fallacy" intruder. This is a person who seeks to use faulty logic to convince you about any given condition they want you to agree with. You need to learn the fifteen logical fallacies in order to deal with this type.

The Pity trap: By appearing weak, a person draws on your sympathy to get something from you.

The Martyr trap: A person appears to be suffering and in pain, again, to appeal to your sympathy in order to get something from you.

Aside from these main points above, there are many "bait" tactics beggars will use to gain something without effort. The paradox, a person will often put more effort into these little traps than just going and earning their way in a fair manner.

The REASON someone puts themselves in a begging position vary, but invariably it is because of a perceived frailty or weakness in themselves.

Often, the person is caught in the "I am not good enough" trap. And as much as I say to be wary of the above taking advantage of you, also be wary that you do not fall into the habit of begging from another.

Right and Wrong are Relative Terms

People believe this is right or that is wrong. The truth is, these terms are relative to your viewpoint.

The entire Western culture insists that ITS way is right. This heritage comes to us largely via the Romans, and the Roman Catholic Church. But before you say this is 'wrong', think of the options.

Without the Catholic church, we might all be riding camels and praying five times a day, or worshipping the descendants of Genghis Khan. The message is, nothing is ideal, nothing is absolute. We simply need to make the most with what we have.

And here is the secret: *When we accept life as it is, we soon discover that whatever state we are in financially, mentally or emotionally, there is always a way to trade up to a better set of circumstances.*

Communication and Trade are the paths to freedom, not begging or borrowing. All traders understand one simple rule; first understand what others need. Then apply this information to create a benefit for yourself and the other person/s.

This is called the Art of NEGOTIATION.

We learn to GIVE and TAKE in order to gain an upper hand in dealing with life. We learn the ART of NEGOTIATION in order to get what we need and want. In other words - ASK NO FAVORS but EXPECT Fair Trade. Therefore:

1. Ask no Favors.

2. Make No Promises.

3. Give nothing away that you need and give everything away that you don't. (But first see if someone will pay you to take it away)

4. Use tact, and trust that the winds of life will bring you to your destination.

This Forth Law is not so difficult to grasp. In essence we are saying that we need to be careful of the little hooks we find in between our agreements with others. So, what is the agreement written in between the ethical lines we draw?

Am I 'giving' you these words to garner your respect? Or do I just give it?

Neither, I am trading this information for money. I sell you this book as an exchange of energy.

Get it? *Fair trade is no man's loss.*

A Harsh Lesson

In Australian Aboriginal Society, anthropologists initially believed the Native populations were total communists because it seemed to them that no one owned anything and everything was shared. Nothing could have been further from the truth.

Everything was shared, yes, but subtle emotional and mental records were kept of EVERYTHING. If you borrowed an artifact or thing of power from one family, you may have it in your house for a whole lifetime. But your descendants were expected to repay this gift with one of equal value. An anthropologist discovered this when he spoke to his native elder friend about all these relics he had been given. He said, "You are so kind, what can I give you in return?"

The headman replied "I have indebted my family for generations to give you these things. I did this because I believe it will help my people and my race. It is not possible for you to repay this debt. But if you help my people survive, you have repaid me."

The anthropologist was deeply shocked. This native culture has a notion of a MORTGAGE? When he started asking specific questions, he began to see that their ENTIRE CULTURE was based on trade. Not just of goods, but of thoughts, feelings, physical articles, and experiences.

Doing a DANCE at a particular meeting may be a form of repayment for some event from your GRANDFATHER's time. This is why lineage and territory were an integral part of Land Rights. It was all part of a very delicately balanced state of agreement. This is also why most Native Societies become utterly and irreversibly ruined by intervention of any sort.

The anthropologist's recommendation to the Government of the time was that this was a far more involved culture than anyone imagined and that the whole area where these people lived should be locked up and kept from development until the process was better understood.

Of course, the man was ignored and the 'natives' were rounded up and taught to 'behave', largely by missionaries. Thus, aboriginal culture was all but destroyed, and many of the members of those societies are still wandering around, completely lost. This is an example of how evil placing a Should on someone can be. Please do not do this to yourself.

> *Contemplation: You may be out there thinking you are catching a fish, but have you considered it may be thinking exactly the same thing about you?*

FIVE:

Keep your Teeth Honed

Si Vis Pacem, Para Bellum
(If You Want Peace, Prepare for War)

This is a short and easy rule to grasp. If you want less trouble in life, be prepared for a fight. Despite all good Rats being demure and shy, there are times when we need to protect our space. To do this, we need to keep our teeth honed. This means keeping ourselves fit and ready for war.

This also means saying what needs to be said. Defining your boundaries. Keeping your workspace clear of clutter. The point of Rule Five is that when someone knows you are ready and willing to do so, you rarely HAVE to bite.

We prepare for a fight in order to avoid argument. It is like holding a nuclear arsenal; It works because you have it, not because you use it.

Robert McNamara (Secretary of Defense during the Vietnam War) was initially joking with his now famous 'Mutually Assured Destruction' theory. (MAD) This was the principle of holding a big enough arsenal to make absolutely certain that if YOU went down, so did your enemy.

It really was MAD, but this was the nature of the nuclear arms race. Billions were spent on developing a capability for worldwide destruction – supposedly for the express purpose of never having to use it.

Completely MAD, yet it has worked so far!

The US Government SPENT the Soviets into bankruptcy as they both played Economic, Social, and Environmental 'Russian' Roulette. Mad, absolutely. Yet, because the teeth WERE honed, neither party would advance against the other for fear of their bite.

Do I support the nuclear armament race? Not at all. It is a Thucydides Trap. Only a fool LIKES this madness but the reality is, what are the options?

It's the old Boy Scout motto: *Be Prepared*. Keeping your teeth honed means being READY, ABLE, and TENACIOUS. I know, a RAT acronym. But for a Rat, this means far more than just being prepared to fight, it means being prepared to live. Ready, able, and tenacious means ready to move at a moment's notice, ready to grasp the opportunities life provides. Being willing to do so means you embrace change. Being able to do so means you are not carting excess baggage. It also means you DO look the gift horse in the mouth and make sure it is not a Trojan.

On the practical side of things this means you fix the hole in the roof on a sunny day, not when the rain starts to fall. Keeping those teeth honed means you have thought about, and prepared for, a variety of scenarios. It is simply better to have everything you need in place BEFORE you step out the door.

A perfect example of a failure in this regard was how Napoleon sent troops off to Russia without proper food or clothing. The Russians just retreated and let them freeze and die.

Hitler did exactly the same thing. He went in thinking things would be easy, but it took far longer than expected and his army was caught unprepared. Therefore his assault failed. In simple terms, Russia was the end of his dreams.

We can think ourselves fortunate because if he had NOT taken on Russia he would have had time to develop the science of Nuclear Bomb and ICB's and we might all be speaking German.

But how DID Hitler get so far so quickly into France? Hitler got his foothold in Europe because the teeth of the leaders had grown blunt. Europe was completely unprepared for war. People laugh at the 'Peace in our time' accord now, but back then everyone cheered Chamberlain for 'preventing war' and ignored the dire pronouncements from Churchill.

Churchill was ABUSED in the media when warning of the dangers they all faced.

If we are not prepared to face the obvious and deal with consequences, we will end up writing a large reality check to cover the cost of our avoidance.

Avoiding a fight is one thing; it is wise to duck a punch. But not being ready to fight back is another thing entirely. People SENSE when you are unprepared, and thus vulnerable. You WILL suffer as a result. But keep your teeth sharp, your wits clear, your

vision undulled by compromises, then your potential enemies will look for an easier target.

Life deals us a hand. Whatever it is, our job is to make the most of it. But a card deck is limited. It is an "all facts are known" situation. You KNOW the cards to be dealt will have to be a heart, spade, club, or diamond. Fifty-Two cards, each with a specific value and suit. Real life appears more random, and it is as it has more cards and options – but the same principles apply. Keeping teeth honed will always help.

"Who Gives a Rats?" (Third book in this series) will assist in understanding the 'card deck' better, but as an overview, we have a limited number of thoughts and emotions – Like an alphabet, the Twenty-Six letters of English can combine to make over six million words.

Each word we speak is a condensation of thought and emotion. SIT means a very specific thing we all understand. But what does it means to your dog? When I say SIT to my dog, I am not telling him to sit, I am telling him to obey. I am putting a SHOULD on the dog, and if it obeys, it gets rewarded.

This is what politicians and media have done to YOU. You have been trained to obey specific commands. The trigger words are many, but 'communism', 'socialism', 'red peril' are common enough words – but what they MEAN is SIT. You are meant to sit and pay attention. Each country has its own code of commands issues via media and it is all part of the general programming of the populace.

Keeping your teeth honed means you are aware of these buzz words, and be prepared to deal with the emotional baggage they imply.

We have an entire movement to the ultra right worldwide at this point in time. There is a reason why. It is an instinctual reaction to these mind controls.

The entire MAGA business in the States is, at its core, a rebellion against the buzz words. I am not saying I agree with it, but I do understand, a huge number of people are struggling to get out from under the heel of convention. Will it work? No – because they are not obeying the Rat Rules.

You ask: *How are the Rat Rules being ignored?*

The reasoning in the MAGA movement lacks a coherent basis. To Whit: I am off to a convention because I want to break away from convention!

You cannot break the laws of reason or logic and expect things to survive for long. We go a while on emotional energy, but once the driving force is exhausted, there will be nothing left.

So, how CAN we break away from convention and survive? It is the Thoreau Quote: *"Any man more right than his neighbors constitutes a majority of one already."* The real question is how to see more rightly! Again, learn to see the obvious. This usually means we have to look through the illusion dancing before it.

However, that is just the start point. Real freedom comes when we shift our attention to a smaller deck of cards, the pictures at the core of our psyche: The Core Karmas! These are the base line concepts of right and wrong , etc. that you inherited as a child.

The Rat Rules are the Wild Cards in your deck – they break all the imposed regulations and beliefs, and instill a higher reality into your moment.

Just employing Rule One: *"It's not about me!"* removes most of the negative influence of media and social conditioning. That is a massive advantage.

If someone assaults what I have written with poor reasoning and shouts, "You are a HERETIC!" - Well, my automatic reaction is, "How so?"

Curiosity is one of our WILD CARDS. We already know they are talking about themselves and their beliefs – I have no need to defend, or argue – Instead, I can ask them to extrapolate.

And here is the rub: When an argument is based on false reasoning, when questioned, it demonstrates large gaping holes. These are your escape routes.

AKA - Rule Six: *Always have a bolt hole.*

Things to Note:

How well you play the game is not necessarily about the cards you get dealt, but in how well you read the people around you. See the obvious, and you can make a calculated guess at what they might have.

In Poker, I win hand after hand with no real cards because I allow people to believe they are behind. Here is the secret: *What I will choose to do in a game depends on how sharp I feel the opponents teeth are.*

The decisions THEY make are likewise often determined by how sharp they think MY cards are.

The Soviet Union deferred American aggression for DECADES because they looked ready to go to war.

The US military genuinely believed the Russians were far better armed and more ready for war than they were. What defeated the Russians was a political system that destroyed personal incentive. Capitalism did not win, the USSR lost the war from within.

Russia was bankrupt.

Boris Yeltsin caused the breakup of the Soviet Union because of an American supermarket in Miami – He saw first hand that there were no shortages in the West – everyone was well fed. He went back and demanded faster change than Gorbachev was willing to commit to. To force change, Yeltsin convinced Belarus and the Ukraine to pull away. He then disbanded the Communist Party, Gorbachev's base of power. This is what caused the collapse of the Soviet Union.

If you want to win, you first have to win the war within yourself. Another reason to keep your teeth honed is to continually remind yourself that you are ready, willing, and able to fight the good fight.

Remember Star Wars and how the Jedi had grown complacent? They let down their guard because they thought the war was won with the Sith. Well, thank goodness they were lazy because all those movies would never have been made otherwise!

The Rat Rules

SIX:

Have a Bolt Hole

Question: How do you make the Gods laugh?
Answer: Tell them your plans.

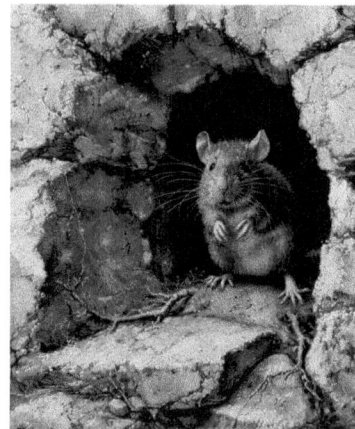

The Mystic Rat Says: It is far more difficult for a serious man to put his tongue in his cheek than it is for him to enter into the Kingdom of Fun.

It's an old story. No matter how you plan, no matter how well you organize things, the "X" factor can and will occur. This is the time and place when the Gods come and put a big red "X" right across all your hopes and expectations. Thus: You need an exit strategy for every plan you make. We all know the saying: *For every door that shuts another door opens*. But have you heard the flip side of this? *For every Door that opens another door shuts.* Either way, CHANGE is about, and we need to be ready for it.

When astronauts take a journey into Space, there is always an escape pod. Every ship at sea has a lifeboat. High rise buildings must have a fire escape.

We need this in our life. Like carrying an umbrella in case it rains, we NEED to have a place or a situation we can retreat to, if needed. This means we can RELAX and not worry so much about consequences.

I met an old Drunk in the streets of Sydney many years ago. It was a perfect sunny day, yet he was carrying an umbrella. I asked him why, and he said: *"I always have an umbrella! When you live on the street, an umbrella is worth more than money in the bank. It keeps the sun and the rain off you and it also has a sharp point which you can use to protect yourself."*

When he had his umbrella, he felt safer and more at ease in his difficult circumstances. Kerry Packer, the Australian Businessman, always had One Million Dollars in GOLD in a safe in his office. Why? If everything fell over, he would have his GOLD, because it can always be traded for what you need.

There was a second reason, which highlights what a perfect Rat the man was. He put that One Million Dollars of Gold into petty cash. Strange, you might think? As the price of gold went up, he took some of the gold, just enough to keep the net value of funds in petty cash at one million dollars. Tax-wise and according to the books he retained one million dollars in petty cash. After two decades, he retained only 22% of the original gold, but it was still worth one million dollars. (He also had a fully equipped B&D room behind his office, but that's another story.)

58

And then the impossible happened, the price of gold crashed. What to do?

There was a huge shortfall looming. This is when it gets interesting, the gold gets STOLEN from the safe in his office. It has an insured weight of 285 Kilos (628 lbs or roughly 10,000 ounces = 25 standard gold Bars). Police are pretty sure they know who did it, but can't prove a thing. No one gets charged, yet of course, Mr. Packer is fully insured for the WEIGHT of gold. The market value was now worth 5.6 million dollars.

How can this be? He has taken away most of that gold and sold it over the years? It was perfectly OK with the accounting because the weight was registered when it was put in. The law did not require the gold to be WEIGHED each year, only that the VALUE had to stay the same. I know this story because his bondage mistress told me; otherwise it was one of the close-lipped secrets of Australian society.

"What a RAT!" you say? True, but you have to admire how he manipulated the legal status of his gold.

What are you using for YOUR safety net? Is it superannuation, a second house, money in the bank? These are all perfectly normal ways to protect our financial interests, but what about your emotional and mental safety? What are you doing to protect your mental health? It is something few people think about.

If all you are doing with your life is planning for a safe future, you are already half-way to insanity.

Most people squirrel stuff away for their future financial safely, building the nest egg, as they say. But they can become so locked into this they lock the door to fun. We can relax in retirement, can't we? Well, no! If you have lived a life cutting off the flow of fun, retirement will just be you doing more of it.

A good friend of mine, diagnosed with liver cancer, was staying with me. He had a tremendous sense of fun and humor, despite his present circumstances. One day he said to me, "You know, I lived my life hard. I had a great time. I have no complaints my time is coming earlier than most. I had fun, I spent everything. There was no pension plan, no real estate, no superannuation, and I was starting to get worried what was to happen in my old age." He looked at me quite seriously, then his serious face paused. A huge, cheeky smile spread across his dial. "The good news - now I got nothing to worry about!"

Fear is the mind killer. Fear poisons our sense of well being. It cuts us off from connecting to the life force within. Fear is a mental health issue. It stops us living in the present. Under the rationale of building a safety net for old age, fear can shut us out from happiness.

We can start to think that hiding from life is safety, that cutting off fun will protect us. Let me promise you one thing: *DISCONNECTING is not a good safety net.*

And we disconnect in a hundred little ways: Sweep the dirt under the rug. Stay in a job you hate. Chew down anti-depressants rather than do something useful. Watch TV rather than the sunset. Talk about nothing and go around filling your personal holes with space rather than reading a book that fills your heart.

So many life avoidance techniques!

Saving for old age will get you many things, but if this is based in fear, that that is what you have in the savings bank. Old age comes and you discover your fears cannot buy happiness or contentment.

The ONLY Reality is NOW

A perfect example of the present state of social disconnect are the reality shows: All those people pretending to be nice while they are competing for a prize. All that apparent laughing and joking hides the fact that they exist to extinguish your hopes. And the drama! It is manufactured with people playing mind games round the clock!

I spent most of my early years avoiding exactly the type of person you see on these shows. Why would I want to watch them? These so-called reality show oppose the natural flow of life. Big Brother, Survivor, etc. are all based on a DISCONNECT.

There is only ONE door that opens and that is the Exit. These show are really about doors closing as you get evicted. Life is NOT like this! LIFE is all about growth and new openings. Real Life opposes everything Big Brother stands for.

If you are reading this, you are human, and you are alive. But are you LIVING? Are you having a great life? Are you waking up to welcome every day?

The concept of rivalry, comparison, or strife is part of a Death Wish. Laughter, fun, and joy are a Life Wish. Which do you prefer? The essence of a fulfilling life lies in laughter, sharing, and caring.

When our focus is solely on the binary of victory or defeat, we detach ourselves from the present moment. Indeed, life comes with its share of risks and challenges that may sometimes require us to make swift decisions and changes. That's why we prepare for such eventualities.

However, an obsession with WINNING can rob us of the joy inherent in the journey.

To Play is to Risk

Eminem sang, in the song, Losing It: *"The Moment, you own it, you better never let it go. You got one shot, do not miss your chance to blow."*

People think he is talking about confidence, courage, beating the odds. No, this is about PLAY. You got this moment, you got opportunity, take it! Play the Game!

But what if it all goes wrong! Safety First! – This is why we have a bolt hole. It gives us room to play.

Risk-taking is not the opposite of the Bolt Hole – it is its natural complement. Despite our best efforts, sometimes the way forward doesn't happen. We make our plans, choose our path, yet no door seems to open. Perhaps we say, "To hell with it" and just leap into the dark, trusting that life will in some way hold us up.

We experience a surge of adrenaline. We feel a thrill. It's exciting! However, the key to taking risks is not to make a blind leap UNTIL a safety net is in place. This approach allows you to safeguard your interests while STILL having a good time.

Having a bolt hole means you CAN run a risk.

Living a life completely safe from RISK is to excommunicate yourself from living. Yet living a life where you risk EVERYTHING on a roll of the Dice or the fall of the cards is another form of disconnect.

It comes back to, "nothing too much". Risk is great. It helps get your heart racing every once in a while, but cover your bases. Get yourself an umbrella of sorts.

Things DO go wrong and if they do a good RAT is prepared to drop everything and RUN when needs be. As a result, they ALWAYS make sure there is one door that remains open in case they need to get away in an emergency. The only risk here is a loss of face, which is no loss at all to a true Rat.

The Power of Questions

We may find ourselves in a situation where we are cornered with no escape. We may have a bolt hole, but we cannot get to it – the way is blocked. You have to find an escape hatch, and the way you do this is by asking questions.

I gave a pretty hitchhiker a lift home one day, many years ago, and she invited me in. Well, she WAS pretty, and I had little else to do, so I went in – only to find it was full of fanatical born-again Christians. They were quite aggressive, demanding to know if I accepted the Lord Jesus as my personal savior.

I had a distinct sense they were not going to let me go until I joined. That sense was accented by the locking of doors, and seven men standing around me. Now, perception is everything – HOW we see and how we shape others to see, can save our lives. In this instance, I listened intently to what he had to say – then when he was finished, I looked very serious, as if I was considering things deeply.

Then I started asking questions. "So, you truly believe that the Lord knows all, he knows why I am here, he knows why you are here, everything?"

Of course they agree. "And if this is the case, The Lord will know and understand that I have a degree of doubt. And I am sure you have possibly felt doubt before, yet through that you came to this place of deep security, yes?"

Of course, they all agree. "So you will understand that BECAUSE the Lord is great, BECAUSE God is great, that when I walk out of here, he will understand my doubt. He will let me come to the logical end of my questions and when the answers come, as you know they will, that it is time for me to turn about and come straight back here, then this is what I will do, yes?

The head guy looked at me quizzically. It made so much sense, he could not disagree, but he wanted to – I mean, they had a live one, can they just let him go? But he could see his brothers nodding in agreement – The logic was flawless.

So they let me go. Oddly enough, the Good Lord never did turn me around to go back there. I am sure you are as surprised as I am about that. But I DID receive a very important message: Use questions to find your path to freedom. Asking questions stretches the persons reality, elongates it with reason – and soon enough, the holes in the logic will appear.

The Mystic Rat Says: Imagine how much worse is the fear of loss of face for a person wearing two of them.

Bubbles of Truth

Truth comes floating our way in bubbles of thought. Often hidden in feelings and beliefs, these bubbles have to be popped if they are to reveal what truth is inside them. Likewise, you have to pop all your hopes, dreams and fears if you want to find the secret hiding within.

SEVEN:
Do Not Expose
Your Vulnerabilities

Invulnerably vulnerable
I wait upon my wall and ask:
Do I open my gate to this?

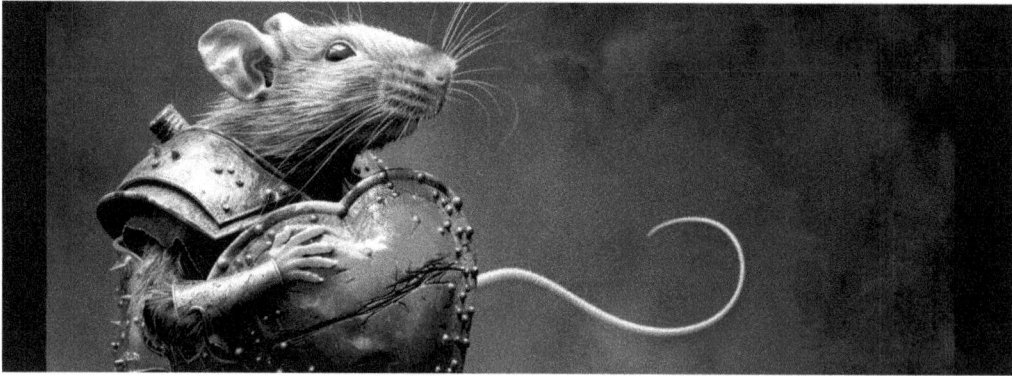

This is a difficult rule to grasp, more so than you might imagine. It all seems so obvious, yet in working with Rule Seven, you will unearth a monstrous reality – that every part of you is vulnerable in some way. The first step is with knowing what our vulnerabilities are and what we are protecting. Most do not protect their true center, while they erect barricades and go to war over things that are essentially a nonsense.

Yes, we all need to protect ourselves, we all have vulnerabilities, but most of us build defenses around useless things, like: points of view, false beliefs, and wrong thinking.

We defend unnecessary issues like: prestige, how we look, or what we believe. Worse, we defend groups and causes that are unrelated to us. Look at Facebook, where you find so many arguing over nothing while their genuine self dies the death of a thousand cuts.

To follow Rule Seven you need to know where you are vulnerable. So first, we must know what we need to protect. Once we discover where and what our vulnerabilities are, then we take steps to protect what matters. This is much harder than it sounds.

For example: We NEED love and compassion in our life, but do we value this? Many see this need as a sort of weakness. If we do not protect these soft virtues, we may find that the iron boots of reason will trample on them. In doing so, we lose a piece of what it means to be human. Worse, we lose our connection with NOW.

Is being Vulnerable a Bad thing?

Vulnerability, by the very nature of the word, is the ability to be vulnerable. It seems wrong, but when you understand that your so-called weak points are where compassion and kindness enter into your world, it will make more sense. You very much need to protect this space. More than this, we need to cherish this space.

Our vulnerabilities are found hiding inside our needs. So first up: Do you understand your needs?

Let's look at the obvious; we need oxygen, water, food, shelter – Every living thing needs to protect these essentials. In assessing what is most vulnerable, look at how long you can live without it. This makes it very easy to define priorities. Obviously, we need oxygen first. We die in minutes without it.

You may laugh, but I met a fellow who rode a bicycle 'for health' in LA. He had passed out three times on the freeways, from all the pollution. He learned to carry an oxygen bottle. So where are you VULNERABLE? What needs defending?

Our needs will tell us: air, water, food, and shelter. Without these we will not live, and to protect these vulnerabilities we need to work, or a way to provide cash to live. Everyone knows we all need this – It is just common sense: these are not vulnerabilities we must hide, as they are common to every soul.

But what happens when an unscrupulous employer learns that you NEED your job to cover a mortgage, and seeks to take advantage of you? You need to recognize predators in your environment, and protect yourself from them. But you NEED that job!

Well, why did you advertize this? If you kept to yourself, minded your own business, and took care to not advertise a weakness, then the would-be predator does not see you. They are looking for an easy meal, so make sure you don't dress up as food.

Kamit: the Law of Silence.

Only open the heart to people you trust. This is Kamit: the Law of Silence. It means to speak what is necessary, when it is necessary. It means to observe your surroundings before you engage with it. Find a perfect inner silence where all things are made clear.

When a person talks in terms of being a victim, of finding him or herself in difficulty, of needing money to survive, they are opening the door to predators. Loose lips sink ships.

Keep the door shut to the wolves. Never expose vulnerabilities, never call yourself a victim.

But we all have interactions with work colleagues, social media: places where we intersect with the world. How can we stay silent and not speak when our opinion is called for? What happens when the boss asks how we are going? Obeying the Law of Silence is knowing WHAT to say, and WHEN to say it.

What about promotions, needing to be seen? If people hold a poor image of us, it can undermine promotion prospects, social opportunities, etc.

Well, better silent and be thought a fool than open your mouth and prove it. We need to protect any area where conflict or judgment can arise. HOW you do this is personal, but at the same time, all these interactions must obey Rule One: It's not about you!

It's not about YOU

First step in learning the Law of Silence is to apply the very first rule, "It's not about you". This means to take nothing personally – this is essential if we are to understand Rule Seven. It does not mean to need nothing from others; it does not stop our needing to be part of the tribe. What it means is that when we stop taking things personally, we no longer need to defend the meaningless things that are not essential.

Sadly, people take things personally, and are full to the brim of protecting useless stuff. People will argue to the death over whose God is best, what race is best, what country is best, whose opinion is best. Who cares? In ten years, will it matter? If not, do not waste time or energy to defend it.

More importantly, are we leaving the truly important things vulnerable? Appearances can't keep you warm at night, so pay attention to the things that do. Partner, family, the pets: These things are FAR more important to protect than any opinion.

Sadly, so many people spend so much time defending how they look, or arguing over trifles.

The health of the Inner Child is diminished with every stupid conflict we engage in. Worse, when we are so busy defending the programmed nonsense in our head, we do not see the predators circling.

These problems arise when the "shoulds" are in charge. This causes the natural self and the spiritual self to divide. The energy of soul and the social individual no longer work in harmony – they become DISCONNECTED. This is a target for predators

Our intuition no longer whispers to us, which makes us easy prey. If we followed our instincts, we would protect ourselves far better, but we do not. We follow the dictates of society, with its polite correctness, and we become vulnerable to every predator who, in the modern world, is after our money rather than our lives.

How to Pick a Predator

If you don't want to be eaten you have to know how to pick a predator. The easy way is to show them a wallet full of money. They will instantly pretend to be your friend and go out of their way to separate you from that money. They will look for vulnerability, a soft spot for them to target.

I watched this first hand. In a company I was involved with, the fellow in charge of raising the money would be on the phone, laughing at some joke, then hang up. I asked what the joke was, he said, "Terrible. I only laugh to keep the fish on the line."

This is what predators do, make you feel welcome, appear to open their hearts, and bring you into a circle of trust. The goal is not your well being, it is theirs.

Someone with exposed vulnerabilities is easy meat – you need someone to laugh at your terrible jokes? Sure. Ha ha ha. Now can I have your money?

People who want your money without a fair exchange are predators. And sadly, this is 95% of most professions. The doctor who barely listens as he writes you a script, he/she is a predator. The mechanic who charges that extra hour, another predator. The solicitor who bills a few extra hundred for a three line letter, yet another one.

We have to learn to protect ourselves, and here I will offer some advice that may surprise you, and it may change your life!

One of the best ways to avoid predators is to be both interested and interesting. It is curious to me, but I rarely get overcharged for services. I came to understand this was because I took an interest in the person doing the work, and found them interesting.

Accordingly, they found ME interesting. And as everyone wants things to be interesting in their life, they act in a way to keep you around. Usually this means charging you the right price.

The Wooden Leg

I knew a man who had a wooden leg. It was very obvious, and people would stare, so to have a little fun and to ease the social tension, he would tell them any story that came to mind about how it happened.

"Surfing, Great White took it."

Another day it would be, "Vietnam, booby trap." The truth was, it got infected and was surgically removed.

One day I asked him if he was worried that he might tell a person two different stories, and he smiled, saying, "All people want is a good story. It is boring to tell them the truth, but if they want me to be boring, I will tell them the truth."

I got the message, the wooden leg was a weakness, but he painted it as a strong point – by making it interesting he changed the dynamic, and thus the interaction people had with him. He made a benefit out of his disadvantage.

This is an excellent way to hide a vulnerability.

The fact you are interesting means you are more aware than the dull person – Predators go for the weak and vulnerable, and bypass people who look like they will fight back. (Rule Six: *Keep your teeth honed*. This is an integral part of Rule Seven.)

In the direct sales industry, salesmen go to your home to quote and sell you on whatever – home improvements, vacuum cleaners, encyclopedias, etc.

You are taught to look for "wood ducks" – people who will sit still and do what you tell them to do.

People with interesting stories, who appear alive and awake, these ones are hard to sell to – so you go for the easy marks: People who will feel you like them because you laugh at their terrible jokes.

I asked a very successful car salesman how he managed to sell so many cars. He said, "It's easy – see this new car, just open the door, then shut it."

So I do as asked. "Do it again, just open and shut it, listen to that new car door sound."

I do it once more, and he asks me to do the same thing a THIRD time. I looked at him, and said, "I have done that enough."

"See, you are not a person I will sell a car to. The majority of people will do as they are told, and if they open and shut that door three times, they will buy a car from me."

So the message, don't be a bunny. If you are not awake to the predators, you will become their supper. Have some teeth, be prepared to bite back, and they will leave you alone. By doing so you do not expose vulnerability.

But most people fear the tradesman and the bill they will present, so they try to joke with them and get on, hopping they will play nice. They may even laugh at your terrible jokes. Trying to hide behind niceness will expose your weak points.

Fear of conflict, concern for loss of face, needing to appear to be right - these are all signals to predators that you are vulnerable. You look like a bunny in the spotlights.

But look like someone who is interesting, who will defend their home and family, who will fight for their rights, then the predators just go for an easier meal.

Do Not Hide

Your very attempt to HIDE can be the signal that will make people look. I knew a fellow who lived in a rental house. He had a Marijuana plant growing in the back yard and was surprised to be given notice of a real estate inspection. He was scared it would be seen, so he decided to HIDE it - But he hid it by attaching plastic red flowers to the bush. What?

I saw this and laughed. I then asked him what on earth he thought he was doing. "I am making it look like a flowering shrub, so they won't see it's a dope plant," the fellow explained.

What could I say? Inspections were about to start. The Dope Plant now stood out like Dog's Balls. It was glaringly obvious that something was amiss and EVERYONE who looked at the house went up to inspect the silly plant with the red plastic flowers. Given his drug paranoia, the poor fellow was a mess by the time it was done.

On the flip side, his neighbor had a dope plant growing in full view in his front yard. But this fellow approached things very differently. He trimmed the illegal herb like a topiary bush, shaping it to a nice round ball. This made his marijuana plant incredibly overt and obvious, yet now it looked like a conventional garden decoration, thus no one was curious as to what it really was.

The BEST way to hide your vulnerabilities is to not hide them. Keep them in open view, but give it a shape or form that is interesting. Trust that few can see the obvious.

Everyone is Vulnerable – Accept it

Everyone is vulnerable in some way - this is a given. We all have a weakness, but this does not mean we need to ADVERTIZE our issues. As one example: Most of us seek to cover up the dark side to our nature – And often with good reason. Maybe you are an alcoholic, and the boss would fire you if he knew, so we hide this reality.

In the wild, predators target a creature showing weakness. So we learn to cover the negatives. Yet, every so often, some little part of us lets us down, and we give away our vulnerable state. In Poker, giving away your position is called a "Tell".

It can be involuntary. If a girl likes a man, her pupils will involuntarily dilate, a man does the same when looking down to see a pair of aces - the eyes widen slightly. Your 'tell' could be a look of disgust as you look down on yet another rubbish hand. But most often our 'tells' are a response to a deep seated need for acceptance.

As a simple example: Many people, as they enter a relationship, feel the need to confess their frailties, or their shortcomings. We tell ourselves we are being honest, in truth, we are being weak. Unless you have a sexually transmittable disease, it is very unwise to introduce a person to your weakness. It is your problem, not theirs.

If you want acceptance, you first have to accept yourself. That way, you don't have to hide things and equally, you don't have to be too open.

By not accepting our issues, we often create worse ones. Many people hide frailty behind arrogance or bravado. Some hide their frailty behind sarcasm and "mean girl' behavior. A narcissist is hiding the fear they are worthless. A small clue: whatever persona a person displays in society is often the opposite of what they feel inside.

People Create Personas to Hide their Fear

I had an uncle, a mean spirited, nasty man. His children lived in fear of him and most people avoided his acerbic, unpleasant sarcasm. Yet very late in life, I visited him, and it was like visiting a happy child. He was bright and smiling, extremely pleasant, and could not be sweeter. On the way out, he noted, "Remember

Uncle Colin?" he asked. I said I did. "You know, I thought him a fool, he didn't care what anyone thought – but you know, he was RIGHT!"

It hit me, all that nastiness was a façade to hide the fear of what others thought of him. How extraordinary! He was covering up a weakness. Then it hit me, this is exactly what we ALL do. There is a reason why Janus, the God of the Romans, was a two-faced God!

Some cover up their weakness very well, most do not. Under a little pressure, they crack. People will try and bluff you all the time, but most cannot sustain it – a few questions, a little close inspection, and they crumble.

If you are nervous in an interview, you are advertising you don't think you are good enough, as one example. But instead of trying to hide the nerves, we can reverse it. When I have a big hand in poker, I do the opposite of hiding - I say words to the effect, "I love this bit - where you just don't know what's going to happen next. It's what Poker is all about! This is the fun part of the game."

Then before you go to make a large bet, stop - hesitate, and say, "But do any of you have Aces?" Just watch, their faces will tell you everything. You USE your nervous energy to wake up THEIR feelings of frailty.

For most, life is stress and it is competition. Be it love or sport or business, people love to win and fear to lose. In this harsh game, a nervous person is read as fearful - Give off fear, you will be seen as weak.

So, most players in life try to cover up their fear – they play it cool: The tough guy, the ice queen, etc. Each to their own, but for me it is not a whole lot of fun. I look at people with stiff backs and pursed lips and know they are trying to hide their weakness. As a result, I tend to prod them till they crack. Having fun is half the fun, people. I am here to live, to play, to laugh, and to enjoy my day.

For me, fear is nervous energy inverted. I need to REVERSE this, I need it to flow out and become a positive.

So I test the waters. I ask questions, make jokes, up the ante' as they say. In social circles, in poker games, as well as in the workplace, the person who seems the most confident wins the day. And what happens in the mind of those interacting with you? In a poker game, everyone at the table is trying to read you, to find vulnerability. Are you excitable because you know you will win, or are you talking because you are afraid?

Doubt creeps into their mind. The wheels start to turn. By letting go of YOUR need to hide a fault, you often expose theirs, and they fold.

Reverse Psychology

There is also the flip side. Sometimes you WANT something to be found and the best way to do it is to pretend it is a secret. A perfect example of hiding what you want to be found and displaying what you want to hide is found with a friend of mine who used to sell things door to door.

As a salesman in their home, he would drop a ten-dollar bill on the carpet when quoting for some job. In front of them, he would pick it up and say, "Goodness, is that your money? I mean I wish it were mine because I love money, but I have to be honest and admit it isn't MINE!" He then gives it to the potential customers. And what is more, they always take it!

How does giving away money help the salesman?

1. By showing the money, then saying it isn't his means that he is telling the customer that he is incredibly HONEST.

2. This HIDES the fact he wants their money even when he openly says he loves money and he wishes it were his.

3. He WANTED the people to find the 'hidden' surprise because it meant that at the end of his presentation he KNOWS they have a $10 deposit.

(The greatest excuse people make for NOT deciding on something is that they have no money, not even enough for a deposit)

4. But the real reason he dropped the money? He unearthed the customer's GREED.

I am not saying he was right to act in this manner, or that he was a good person. The reverse, he was a predator, but this helped him survive. How does it apply to Rule Seven? Everything is about survival. If he went in and said, "Look, I am broke and need you to buy my stuff," he would be tossed out the door. He was obeying Rule Three, not being a beggar or a borrower, by learning to negotiate.

Curiosity is the Key

If you want to succeed, be curious, create curiosity. Imagine a child that won't eat the food in front of him. You cannot convince a child to eat what they don't want to eat, so the trick is to do the opposite.

NEVER place new food on their plate. I always put what I wanted them to try on MY plate. Children are curious creatures and invariably they ask what the food is. Now try to convince them they DON'T want it.

I say, "It's grown up food. You wouldn't like it." By showing, but then placing out of reach, I reduce the possibility of rejection and increase the desirability.

Almost all children say, "Can I try it?" You have to object for a little bit, but eventually, you give in, and say, "OK, but I am telling you, you won't like it."

Most often the kids find they LIKE it. Why? *Because they DISCOVERED it!* Everyone likes the taste of discovery. If you put it on their plate, you are forcing it on them. But show it, then take it away, and you develop curiosity.

CURIOSITY is the secret power that will give you success with Rule Seven.

Curiosity creates attention, attention creates interest, and interest creates desire. How does this reduce your vulnerability factor? It is sleight of hand. We are learning to DISTRACT in order to PROTECT. You get people curious about what you have, what you are doing, etc. Then, while their attention is on one thing, you slip in what you want to say, sell, or bargain with.

If you want to make something disappear, you get people to look at the other hand. You then drop whatever you are holding and no one will notice.

In Poker, winning is a process of getting more chips. You get more chips by convincing people to fold their hands, regardless of what you may be holding. You win in the mind more than with your cards.

If you have an unbeatable hand, you don't want anyone to know it - You want to slow play and see if someone will get excited and bet in. If you have a weak hand, you want people to imagine you have the winning cards, and you do this by maybe bluffing with a big bet on a high card that hits the deck.

Now if someone has a great hand, you will lose because they will call your bluff - But the odds are that they won't and your subterfuge will get you chips. We look at the odds, what we have, and how other people are playing: then we can work out the best way to disguise our vulnerabilities.

This is true in all areas of playing the game of life – Never admit your vulnerabilities. Never sit on the fence when you are vulnerable. Never put yourself in a position of begging. Never try and give something to people unless they ask for it.

The best way to survive this world is to smile, be confident, and ask questions about how others feel or think about any given thing.

Friendly curiosity is an almost impenetrable armor.

The Mystic Rat Says: *Stop SHOULDING on your self! Stop apologizing for the fact that you are ALIVE.*

EIGHT:
Pay Attention to Your Brother's Activity
(But not their business)

This is a simple rule – it follows on from keeping one eye open, but in this it is specifically about paying attention to the world around you, where issues that might affect us could be hiding.

I had an odd dream. A snake was hiding in the grass, wanting to bite me. I woke up and wondered what it might mean, literally, a snake in the grass. I had a private loan out to cover costs during a divorce - Loan solicitors, they are snakes in the grass! Sure enough, I dig and they were trying to get an extra $5K out of me.

This is seen in a stark truth every day, all around the world. People are trying to get everyone else's money. If you don't stay awake to the game, you will lose yours. This notion of looking after your neighbor is all well and good IF you are certain your neighbor is not out to get you. This is why we pay attention to our brother's activity, to work out whether we are in a safe zone, or a war zone. For this reason ONLY, you need to remain aware of what your Brother does.

You are not your brother's keeper and you are a fool if you trust him to be yours. At the same time, you do not need to know his business beyond the point where it may interfere with yours. The principle is simple: It does not matter if you get on with your neighbor or otherwise, stay in touch with the neighborhood and listen for what news is on the wire.

This is the only good purpose behind listening to gossip, because somewhere along the line, if someone means you harm you may hear of it. You still have to make sense of the whispers that are in the air, but if you pay attention to the warnings as they come down the wires it can work in your favor.

I had a mad neighbor once – he is a perfect example. I DID listen to the whispers, but they were SO negative I thought, "No one can be THAT bad!"

Well, more fool me for expecting the best of people. In this case, the rumors WERE true, he WAS that bad. I paid the price for not paying attention and in a sense, I broke Rule Ten by Playing the Pope.

The point here is obvious: I could have listened without expectation, rather than observe with eyes and ears that wanted to see and hear the best in everyone.

In the background I was shoulding on myself, saying I should not think badly of others. Maybe so, but in this instance it cost me dearly. It did teach me about Rule Eight, and in due course, also Rule Nine: We pick up, dust off, and start again.

By believing that no one can be that bad, I set into motion a whole series of events that drew me into a web of confusion, suffering, and pain. People really can be sour, unforgiving bastards and we must never forget this. If the message that comes through the wires reads, 'Be careful' - well, BE careful. If the message is, "This is a Saint!" - Be even more careful.

Observe your brothers action, look to see how he does little things. In due course make your judgment on the situation from what seems obvious to you. Remember, giving something more time before you act costs you very little and can save you a lot of grief.

A subset of this rule: Pay close attention to people that surround any project you are intending to enter into. They can and do influence outcomes to a huge degree. Also, aim to keep things tight. You want to minimize the number of players who are in your hand.

We deal with techniques to bring unruly partners and neighbors onto your side of the fence in RATOLOGY TWO. The essential technique is the practice of the old phrase: *Keep your friends close, and your enemies even closer.* If you believe you have a problem in the wings, go out of your way to embrace it, welcome it, bring it close to you. That way the problem believes you are its friend and slowly it will start telling you ITS secrets.

There is a very simple principle: *Avoid conflict situations wherever possible.* If there is a problem in that part of your world, maybe it is easier to just look elsewhere? The principle technique for applying Rule Eight is a matter of keeping one ear to the ground and two eyes open. Look for the obvious and obey the most important subset of this rule: don't be a hero.

The best way to avoid a loss is to sniff trouble out before it arrives. Feel out the players; get the taste of a situation before you move into it.

Always remember the quote from Zeno the Elder: *I have two ears but only one mouth*! LISTEN to what the wires are whispering to you.

Questions are Shields

By not paying attention to potential problems on the horizon, we are effectively asking for trouble. It is important to doubt new players that enter into your life, not to say everyone is bad, but it is fair to say that most people are interested in what is good for them, not you.

A person's reputation, the things they have done before you were part of the scene, these things matter. It is not that these what you will do, but it pays to take time and give a measured response to new events that come into your world.

Ask, and it shall be given!

When we ask to be shown the truth, we are asking to see the obvious. If we stop, listen, and ask questions about a new event in our lives we give ourselves another layer of protection, and who knows, we might get answers that save us from a barrel of trouble.

Questions are shields when properly applied. Asking about a situation before you enter into it – This will equip you with knowledge and help you to defend your ground better than any army can. The correct question can resolve conflict, disarm opponents, and reveal truth. Demanding an answer, rather than hoping for an outcome, gets the best results.

But it pays to remember: Questions can make friends of enemies, yet they can also make enemies of friends – So be circumspect – Your questions have the power to change your life. They polarize situations, and create wealth. But only if you LISTEN to the reply.

Paying attention to your brother's activities, but not their business, is a little like listening to the echoes in a canyon. Listen carefully and you may pick up what life is seeking to communicate. Work with life, listen to its whispers, and it will assist you in innumerable ways.

"The power to question is the basis of all human progress." Indira Gandhi

NINE:
PICK UP, and DUST OFF

This is the Golden Rule of all true RATS. This is the ORDER of the RAT, the one thing that holds everything else firmly onto the Rat Ring of Truth. It is very simple, and again, very obvious: *PICK UP, and DUST OFF*.

There is more to this than meets the eye, however. Of course this means we get up from a fall and get back on the horse - But please read this next part closely, as part two of this Rule is as important as part one.

I also am saying that by keeping one eye open, by being prepared, by keeping our teeth sharp, and protecting our vulnerabilities: ALL the previous rules put you in a position to do what the RAT does best - Spot the diamond in the rough.

Remember: PERCEPTION is what this is all about! See what others do not, and whatever you see, be ready to pick it up, and dust it off. There is an old tale of Alexander the Great taking over an Etruscan city.

Etruscans were known the world over for their ability to negotiate and arrange business dealings in their favor, so Alexander was completely deaf to their entreaties. In fact, he meant to specifically embarrass them, so he packed them off to a worthless plot of land and said, laughing, "Here, I give you this land and all it contains. It is YOURS in exchange for your city."

The old king who was leading the evacuees bowed low and thanked Alexander for his kindness. Then, with a look of surprise, he bent down and picked up a rock that was at Alexander's feet. He dusted it off, revealing a brilliant, HUGE diamond, saying, "Thank you my Lord and Master for the gift of this land and all that it contains."

Of course, he would have palmed the jewel on the way out of the city, but the point was made. You cannot defeat a person who finds OPPORTUNITY and LUCK wherever they go, especially when they create it! Fortuna and Ops, Luck and Opportunity: These were the Gods of the Sabine, the tribe that lived in the district where Rome was built.

They were the only true Gods of the Romans and they remain the twin pillars for success, even today.

How does this apply to you? A simple question: *Are you going to be part of the millwheel, grinding away all day so others can eat the bread, or are you aiming to be a little more independent?*

If you DO want to be free, it's not likely to happen working for the boss, is it? The only reason he employs people is so HE can be free.

However, if you have a sharp eye and keep looking for opportunity there are innumerable ways to make extra cash. One example is the fellow who traded himself up to a HOUSE. He started with some minor thing he didn't need and offered to TRADE.

Eventually, by picking his trades, he ended up with a house. He created his luck by finding opportunity where no one else could. Now THAT is a true RAT.

Some years ago I got back to Australia with a wife and new child. I figured I would have to create some security for the family. So, I started looking around for real estate bargains. The best way for the average person to make money is through Real Estate.

I have a simple rule: Look for something going cheap which you can make more valuable with a little effort. That was my sole credo, so I combed the papers and the agents for cheap property. I was amazed at how much I found. Of course, cheap usually means there is a problem to solve, but that's OK. As long as it was cheap enough to justify the effort required.

Eventually, I bought acreage close to town with a badly run-down house on it. Now: I didn't know how to renovate a house, but I figured by asking questions I would sort it out . I bought the place. It was in bad shape: It even had sections hanging in mid-air where stumps had once been. The real estate agent who sold us the property said it was a demolition problem.

It took three months to make it livable. This meant putting in a kitchen, a bathroom, re-stumping, fixing the roof, re plastering the ceiling, repainting, rewiring sections, polishing the floors - You name it, I did it. It turned from a ruin into something quite cozy.

I had checked out its subdivision potential before buying, and there was a lapsed approval on the place. The first thing I did was to try and revive it and, with a little prodding, we got a small change of the Rules. The five acres that I subsequently chopped off paid my cost for the entire property. This left me some fifty acres that were effectively FREE.

I used some of the money from this sale and put a deposit on a 250-acre place that came up cheap. I then mortgaged that acreage to buy a Federation House that needed repair. How could I say no? It was on a river and it was cheap. After I did this one up, I used THAT house to get a mortgage for another acreage with a sea view that went for a song. Within two years, I had created a brace of properties worth millions.

Unfortunately, it seems that my then-wife didn't like being rich, and she left. That cost a million dollars but by telling convincing stories to the bank, I managed to hold on to some bits of land. (See: The Boringbar War)

I learned something: *It comes and it goes*.

In my life, I have found that anything can and does happen. But when I am connected to my RAT, I see opportunity better and start to make my own luck as a result. A warning: This will polarize things in your immediate social circle and possibly ruffle feathers. Why? Because people tend to get jealous when you seem to be streaking ahead.

C'est le Guerre! This is the cost of being free.

However, I hit a brick wall with the divorce. I had worked hard restoring houses, fixing up old properties, making things work where no one else was interested: but in the end, it was all for nothing, or at least for next to nothing. So what did I do? I got a little depressed, then picked myself up, and dusted off the past.

This was not easy. I was building my own cottage because I could not afford to pay anyone, and I was licking wounds. That house was the one I fell off, which started my understanding that I was working through Roman Karma! (See: I am Roman; Page 21)

In the meantime, I had a child to look after, a house to build, and I had no running water or power. I asked myself why I bothered.

Could it get worse? That's when I saw that it certainly could. At least I had a place to live – I saw I was actually quite lucky! I started to see the possibilities of things before me. I had a creek, a waterfall, and a roof over my head. If I were a native in Bali, this would be heaven!

Plus, this property was a diamond in the rough. I just had to make it more attractive to others and things would work out fine.

I changed my attitude, I picked myself up, I dusted off, and I started again. Within the week I had figured a way to get water to the house, and in a while, I got funds to connect the power.

I am a better person for the experience, so I am RICHER even if just in heart. I did OK in the end. I was persevered and kept myself focused on what was useful. But there were still things I needed to learn, things about self-importance and seeing things clearly.

The Mystic Rat Says: Life provides opportunity; it will not necessarily provide an easy ride.

Examples of how to see things differently:

Change Perspective with Empathy: You believe your father did not love you. But now you choose to see how your father saw things. He struggled to make ends meet. He felt inadequate. He struggled with his own demons.

Your empathy allows you to step back from what YOU feel, and feel for a moment what he went through. A light dawns, he was barely making it through. He felt unworthy of love. It was never about you! You realize what was missing was your love for him. You fill in this emptiness with understanding and the fear and sadness you felt evaporates.

Change How You See Yourself: You felt unworthy. There seemed no specific reason, but the feeling nagged you all your life. Instead of looking at what is wrong, you decide to see what is right in your life. You have achieved much. You have good friends, etc. You count the blessings, you feel the gratitude, and you are released from the sense of unworthiness.

Change How You See Others: A friend has a habit that annoys you. Maybe tapping fingers?

Should you say something? Maybe you need to look at WHY you are annoyed, and consider what is in you that is being aggravated. You make a choice not to judge the situation, and just observe.

You see your friend is repeating his behavior not to annoy you, but because it's a habit. With a genuine curiosity, you gently ask why he/she feels they have to tap the fingers in that way. They may be surprised, they may not have realized what they were doing. A door opens that you can both walk through

Listening to the answer, you realize what they do no longer annoys you.

TEN:
Shoot the Pope

Modesty is only arrogance by stealth.
Terry Pratchett

T he Tenth Rule goes: *SHOOT THE POPE.*
The idea is to kill off the vanity, or sense of
superiority, that is instructing us how to behave –
We are talking about shutting down the part of us
that likes to pretend we are important; that
imagines we are in some way above others.

When we deeply and sincerely practice Rule One,
"It's not about You!" we are letting go of attachments.
This creates a space where we start to see through the
dark mirror of uncertainty and find a place where we
begin to see clearly. But few can let go of their
opinions and notions of importance, and so they
remain stuck in the dark reflection of their life.

*Oh what a gift the giver would give us, to see
ourselves as others see us*! Robbie Burns spoke the
truth! The only way to receive the gift of clarity, is to
understand how you are seen. We must not only stop
looking at ourselves, we must see our self as another
might. A broad hint of what to expect: They won't
think you are the most important person in the room.

Why do I say: Shoot the Pope!

When we meet an arrogant person we all feel a desire
to cut them down to size. When someone acts above

us, or appears condescending, or sounds arrogant, all
we want to do is pull them down a peg or three.

When people act like the Pope it causes them untold
personal problems: no one wants to be your friend,
your partner leaves and takes your money, the boss
fires you for being a smart ass, and people gossip about
what a dick you are. Playing the Pope breaks up
natural communication between equals.

It is just vanity: the most expensive luxury we can
indulge in. Vanity costs us friends, marriages, and
offers no benefit. The paradox of this vice is that it is
the reason we pretend to be important, is because
inwardly we believe we are crap.

Nietzsche said, "God is Dead"

*The Mystic Rat says, "Is God Dead? Fine - Now kill
Your Pope as well."*

How do we do this? It is more important to
understand WHY we do this first – Just as an alcoholic
reaches for the bottle; the insecure person reaches for a
sense of importance to make them feel secure. When
we feel threatened by external circumstances, we tend
to act like everything is fine. It is a bluff, a way to

distract people from our fear. We all do this to some degree, the problem occurs when it becomes a habit.

So how do we wean ourselves off needing to be important? It is both harder and easier than it sounds.

I might add the Paradox of Humility here: The act of pretending you are totally unimportant is ALSO playing the Pope – false humility is the hallmark of the Catholic Church, remember. The true path to deflating your sense of self-importance is very simple – listen to what people are saying. More than this, WANT to know what people are talking to you about.

When you feel the need to speak, stop. Listen to what the whispers of life are saying. You may well feel superior to another person, or you may feel inferior – it doesn't matter. Just listen to what they say, and clarify with them what you heard. Listen with the heart and all of a sudden, people will like you, and want to help.

People who listen are liked – While no one likes a smug bastard. And here is a little secret: *You get much further acting dumb than you do by wanting to show how smart you are.*

A good friend, Paul Smart (Barrister extraordinaire) wins lots of his cases because he acts dumb and allows everyone else to feel superior. He fuels their arrogance and gets the answers he wants from people.

His favorite game is called is "Gilding the Lily". I have seen him question people, almost groveling before them, saying, "Mr. Jones, I know you would not tell a lie. I understand you are an honest man - But seriously, with the testimony you have given, surely you are perhaps GILDING THE LILY … just a little bit? Surely? Perhaps?"

What can the person do? If they agree then they are saying they are lying. If they disagree then the judge KNOWS they are lying. Everyone Gilds the Lily just a bit. Invariably, the person in the witness box denies this and says, "No."

Paul then launches onto the next question with a surprised look and a great laugh, "Oh HO!" he will say, pouncing. "I see Mr. Jones - You are seeking to tell the court that you never even hint at bending the truth, is this what you are trying to tell us?"

People usually then answer, "Well, no."

The trap is set. "What, you admit that you are not telling the truth?"

The person will stammer out that they did not lie in their testimony, not at all - which opens the door for, "So Mr. Jones, you are telling the court that you would never say anything that might possibly put your case into a more favorable light? You are saying you DON'T gild the Lily, never, not at all?"

The person then either gets on his high horse and denies he lied, (thus losing the confidence of the judge) or he admits he lied. The worst outcome is when the person stumbles, saying, "Well, maybe a little."

The amiable Paul Smart then becomes a ruthless eagle diving on his prey. "Oh, so you ADMIT to telling a lie to the court Mr. Jones, yes? This is what you are trying to say, is it?" (And Mr. Smart casts his eye up to the bench with a knowing twinkle as if to say "Another one, Your Honor".)

Everyone is Lying

To a Judge, everyone is lying. It is his job to work out how much or how little. The point is that Mr. Jones is now looking a bigger liar than Paul Smart's client. And that is all you need! You are a nose in front. You do NOT need to appear intelligent, smart or clever. You just need to get out of the firing line and let others stand up and let 'their' egos take the blows for you.

All survivors of war know the safest place to stand is behind a hero. That is what your Inner Pope really is, the part that likes to be the important one, the star, the center of attention. Kill your inner Pope. Why?

Because it is a CENSOR. It will do all it can to stop you finding the true center of your being. It does this by focusing your attention on looking good, appearing truthful, doing the right thing, etc.

Your Inner Pope is the 'shoulder' in your life.

Your Inner Pope is whispering that it is all about YOU. It is not: nothing is about you.

IT'S NOT ABOUT YOU! You are not the best or the worst, the fattest or the thinnest, the smartest or the dumbest, the tallest or shortest – nothing is about you.

By understanding this, we learn the correct way to answer life's little question marks.

Answering Life's Questions

Let's say you are being questioned by Mr. Smart!

What do YOU answer when asked if you have been Gilding the Lily? Rule Ten: do not be the Pope! You can say words to the effect: *"I certainly would not want to say anything to incriminate myself, but equally, if I were to color the facts knowingly and incriminate an innocent man, this I would find equally repugnant. I am saying things to the best of my recollection."*

And here is the important bit: *"But surely it is up to the Honorable Judge to decide how much truth is in my testimony?"*

THIS way of saying things gets you off the hook. You did not play the Pope. You hid your vulnerability. You shifted focus from yourself to the Judge. (A Technique called 'Playing the Third Man' which we deal with in "Who Gives a Rats") You managed to find gold where there was none .

AND you gave yourself a Bolt Hole because you have not said a categorical 'Yes or No'. NB: Categorical answers are known in the legal trade as a hanging statement, and with good reason.

You avoided the bullet yet answered the question sincerely. Let's look at this scenario one more time: Did you cover all the Rules?

1 It wasn't about You. YES

2 Did not Should in your Own Nest. YES

3 Kept One Eye open? YES

4 Asked no Favors. YES ... Left it to the Judge to Decide

5 Kept your Teeth Honed. YES

6 Had a Bolt Hole. YES

7 Did not Expose your Vulnerabilities. YES

8 Paid Attention to your Brothers Activity, but not their business.

ABSOLUTELY YES! This is what got you off the hook here!

9 Picked up and Dusted Off. YES

10 By doing all of this, you have effectively Shot the Pope. You made yourself look humble, and won your legal argument. Well done!

Point Eight is the only tricky one. *Pay Attention to Your Brothers Activity:* Here, you presume that your opponent is going to be telling a lie, and you already know their legal eagles are paid to lie.

But maybe he/she truly believes in the rightness of their cause. They may appear to be very convincing.

The truth is that in matters of being found guilty or innocent, what decides it is how you are seen, and standing there like a Pope will not help you.

By shifting the focus back to the Judge and stating you are doing your best, you are swinging the balance of judgment your way. Unless you are caught out in a blatant lie, the case is already not lost (rather than won) if you are defending a position.

Why is this? In a room full of ugly people, an average looking soul looks beautiful. In a room full of liars, someone who appears to lie less looks the most truthful. But if you act like a Pope, anyone who looks at you will expect perfection and, as that never happens, you will lose.

I might add, another basic principle of being a good RAT comes from Poker. If you have a good hand it is always best to have someone else attack you. If an argument is unavoidable, it is so much easier to defend than to attack. In a court of law the attacking party has to prove guilt, whereas if you are defending, you simply have to indicate a likely innocence.

What about the Court of Public Opinion?

The same thing applies to social groups. Let other people do the parading of peacock feathers. You do not have to appear better than anyone else. You just have to appear OK. No one trusts a Pope and, in the course of time, in any given situation, people will direct their trust and goodwill to the one who appears the most steadfast and honest.

Paradoxically, this is exactly what a Pope is supposed to be, steadfast and honest!

If you want to get by more peacefully in life, sit on the ego, listen to the forces that are at play in the room, and wait for your opportunity. These things will win you more hands than the best cards ever will.

Summary: Remember the Rat Rules and life will go better for you. They put you into a position of strength with every situation you will find yourself in. When properly followed, they create doorways and opportunity where none might have otherwise appeared to exist.

A Note for People with ADHD, or similar

Have you ever considered the possibility that you don't have a disease? Perhaps what you really suffer from is boredom, and perhaps the reason for this is more related to watching people do what they 'should' and some part inside you rebels against this?

If you can learn and apply Rule ONE: It's not about YOU! You may discover an amazing change will come about. The pressure you feel to conform, to somehow fit the square peg into the round hole, will lessen - perhaps vanish!

Society is a field of round holes where everyone is playing golf, but you have a square ball. It just does not work. You feel you must either round off the ball, or leave the playing field. It's just a game. There are plenty of games to play: Maybe take your strange, square notions, and use them to play DICE? Find where your fun is. Take off the grey lens of ADHD and watch your so called autism fade. Understand, you are in a field of color!

It does not matter than you do not conform to the norm, What matters is that we all learn to play with the tool box we were given, and use this to build a door to an expression of our freedom.

77

On Following the Gods of Luck and Opportunity

We speak of the "Rat Race" – the people fighting each other to get ahead, the people inside the wheels of commerce, running to keep it all turning. We are taught to get a good education, a good marriage, a good job, and this will provide a good life. But it doesn't – for most, the net sum of all your life and work adds up to a nagging sense of loss.

How can this be? You followed the rules, you did what was expected – How come you feel hollow inside? Humpty Dumpty is teetering on the edge of the wall, wanting to jump. Why do you feel this?

The answer is simple: You can never rise above the mundane by being part of the mediocre. Following another's expectations, another's rules, and another's path – it only leads you to the state of otherness.

But surely YOU cannot be larger than society, than all the learned men who speak from on high?

Or can you? It all depends on how you see. The acolyte once went to his master, and asked, "How can I achieve mastery?"

His Master nodded, for it was an important question. "Do you see that rock, tell me what you see?"

"I see a rock!: The apprentice answered.

"You think you see what it is, but you only see what it isn't. I see a house, a set of stairs, a statue, a path through the forest. I look at that rock and I ask, '*what is its best purpose?*' And I see the path to completing that purpose. - You look at that rock and see a rock."

Being part of the Rat Race means you opted for the road most traveled. By simple odds, your chance of opportunity on this road is significantly less than if you strike out on your own.

Conclusion: By following the Mos Maiorum, you are saying you do not trust your luck.

Think about this, if you will. Ask yourself if you want Luck and Opportunity in your life, then ask what you are willing to risk to achieve this.

You feeling lucky, punk?

Make PERCEPTION your Start Point

The majority of people live a life in opposition to how we were designed. In the wild world of the caveman, the priority was survival, and this meant constantly looking out, constantly being aware of your surroundings and potential threats.

This is no longer the case – people are raised in relative security, under a fairly solid set of laws to control the behavior of those around you. People rarely fight to survive the day, and those who are raised in this manner do not fit in with society.

Our society and civilization put into place a wide range of shoulds and should nots: religious institutions reinforce these on a daily basis. There are also police and measures of punishment to ensure security in any given society. As a result, people are not looking out for danger.

The conditioning tools of society have made the 'should' and the 'should not' the priority. We live according to how we were trained. We have expectations put upon us, expectations that form the mores of society. These are patterns of belief.

The Pattern by which most people live:

- Belief shapes our focus
- Focus shapes our perception
- Perception shapes our reality

But when you do not make yourself the central point of focus in your life, when you just start LIVING, when you stop the notion of SHOULD, and when you start to wake up to the awareness of your innate ability to just BE – it switches.

When your PERCEPTION comes first in the chain of causation, the pattern shifts:

- Perception shapes our focus
- Focus shapes our belief
- Belief shapes our perception

This seems no great change, the causation chain appears similar, yet it is radically different. Your start point is no longer with what you believe, but in how you see things – What you perceive takes priority. And when this shift happens, you start to see things differently, more to the point, you start to be in charge of HOW you see things.

Imagine the doctor gave you six weeks to live. Imagine how this would change how you see things in your life. Your priorities will shift, your relationships will shift, everything will shift in accordance to this new perception. This is a force feed reversal – the Doctor presents a new reality. This changes perception, which alters focus – and now BELIEF becomes the result.

This is why so many choose to believe in God in their last days. It is also why the Tibetan Buddhist contemplates their death – not for the dying part, but to prioritize our view of living, and of NOW.

We cannot get away from Belief, but we can stop making it our starting point. And before you say Science already does this, or that the rational thinker is not working on belief, this is nonsense. They BELIEVE in rational thinking, they BELIEVE in science. Belief is still the start point.

Make PERCEPTION your start point, and everything changes. The goal is to find the still certain center of your being. In this Omphalos, this belly button of becoming, all you have is NOW and your perception of NOW.

Being Useful

When a person is popular, when they have all the career prospects, marriage prospects, and the "likeability" factor working for them, they are considered to be eligible. In any given society, this is true: Each group has standards by which you are measured and considered worthy.

But standards shift from culture to culture. What makes you eligible in one culture makes you useless in the next. The Tarzan books offer a good insight into this. What made you eligible in England makes you a liability in the jungle. What was considered essential in one society was a waste of time in the next. Polite manners will not help you get food in the jungle, but without them in England you will be frowned on and found unacceptable: So you are not invited to dinner!

But a truly USEFUL person crosses all borders. In the changing social fabric of Europe, one individual was always safe, protected: The Blacksmith. It did not matter who took control of a society, the blacksmiths were protected, because they were useful. Whether it was to make a cannon or a door hinge, the smith was the person who created what you needed.

Yet so many people are like the leaves in Autumn, they do their bit, but when the winter of discontent comes, they fall. This is what happens when you are no longer useful in this world.

Most people devote their time and energy to fitting in, to finding a place where they can earn an income and have a degree of safety.

Which is fine, but when society changes, as it always does, will you be useful? When the power goes out, do you know how to start a fire? Do you know how to hunt for food? Can you build a house? Being useful in changing circumstances means you will survive.

The ability to see the obvious has been the most useful talent in all cultures and throughout all the ages, but not when parasites and sycophants run a society. Shouting out the Emperor has no clothes does not make you popular with the pretenders.

Right at this moment, we have pretense and pretenders everywhere. The recent pandemic is a perfect example; it was already well known by immunologists that a vaccine could not stop the spread of an airborne virus. Yet the obvious was ignored and common sense was trampled on.

Many want to believe a vaccine saved them, and nothing you can say will sway this view. But the excess deaths statistics are now suggesting more people will die from the shot than were saved by it, Could it have been about money and control?

This is a thing to imprint on your heart and mind: The obvious it is anathema to those sewing the seeds of a lie. You will become their enemy, and they will seek to destroy you.

Being Likeable

When a party goes over potential candidates, looking for whom the public will vote for, the decision is always based on who is the most likable. Our position in society is governed by many things; education, ability, responsibility, etc. But unless we are agreeable, unless we appear to be committed to the general status quo, we are unlikely to be chosen by our peers.

The "Peter Principle" by Laurence J. Peters offered the view that in any bureaucracy, a person rises to their level of incompetence. This is true and has a very negative side effect.

In the halls of power, to get ahead people need to lie and pretend to be what others expect.

But the combination of needing to be liked and molding your public image to be likable in order to cultivate promotions – this creates a false persona, a split in the personality, a two faced nature. This is fine if you wish to scale the ladder of success, perhaps even necessary, but it does a person little good in uncovering any degree of lasting happiness.

Being Eligible

The caveman had to learn to 'fit in' if society was to grow. Ergo: You can't hit the other guy with a club and expect everyone to get on. Small, invisible rules of behavior crept in until the peak of rules of Victorian times, where there were books of rules for everyone and for everything.

The proper way to dine, the right words to say to a girl, the correct posture when traveling in a train carriage, the etiquette of passing the port, the rule against lifting your bottom off the chair to reach the salt, and so on. Rule upon rule upon rule, and yet, as a result, England dominated the globe. At its zenith, Queen Victoria reigned over a third of the world, and 25% of the global population. More significantly, the British Government held sway over approximately 35% of global trade.

To ascend in British society, adherence to the rules was mandatory; one had to behave appropriately or face social exclusion. The right hat for the right occasion, a tailored shirt, the correct tie, and suitable attire for each event were all part of the code. The list went on, rule after rule after rule, stifling the spirit and quenching entrepreneurial drive.

It was the machine age, and those that acted like machines did well. Promotion was rarely by merit. What got you ahead was good breeding, social standing, and being of the right class. However, if you were competent AND followed the rules, AND had a decent social standing, then you were considered in the rank of the eligible.

An eligible young man could have his choice between a range of women who would make themselves available to an offer of marriage. He had better job prospects, could join the right club, and meet the right people. Then came the East India Company, and this upended everything.

A man of middling birth and small means could get a position in India. This meant he had a secure income and, by the standards of the locals, he was rich. Indian women made themselves available – Rent was cheap, life was good.

Perhaps opportunity would come his way? A man could find precious stones, ship goods back to England, there were many ways to improve your lot if you grasped the opportunity.

But best of all, you no longer had to be nice. The natives under you could be flogged for the smallest infringement, you could beat your Indian wife with impunity. You took on the role of the imperial overlord and the only persons you had to kowtow to were your immediate superiors. Then, as ordinary people made a fortune, these Nouveau Riche started to return to mother England, buying up country estates, buying up titles, buying up memberships at the best clubs.

Money changed everything. Those returning with pockets full of gold had little respect for the old ways. They were no longer 'nice'. They did not follow the rules, which provided a paradox for the status quo! Presbyterian ethics stated: if you have money, God has approved you.

A bit of a quandary for the old order, who wanted the money from India, but not the inconvenience of these upstarts.

Gold and wealth poured into Mother England from "the Jewel in the Crown of Empire". But with this cash came change. Attitudes had to shift and the invisible rules began to move. Men of impeccable birth and standing no longer ruled the roost, and these 'rule breakers', these wreckers of tradition, barged in to even the most sacred of places, the House of Lords. How so?

Impoverished aristocrats started selling off their lands and titles to the upstarts, and little by little the rigid set of shoulds and should nots got eroded. Change was the new constant!

So was Irony: The early aristocrats in Britain were essentially robber barons, men who rose to power through force of arms. Now money became the great force that overtook all things.

Change is Inevitable

The social rules of Should and Should Not are the little instructions that tell the central computer of society how to act and what to do. Rules are put in place to STOP change. Yet change is inevitable – Therefore the Rules are meant to be broken.

No change means the existing system continues to function, but when new and confusing messages infiltrate the operation; the old program starts to fail. The solution is to write a new program, a new set of rules. The central authority NEEDS a program, a set of instructions, and rather than let itself fail, it adapts.

Imagine that a landlord or factory owner from Victorian England tried to run their business today as they did back then? Now they would be jailed. Today, if a country goes into a lesser developed nation and plunders its wealth, it is seen as a pariah. The delightful paradox: All this was because people made enough money to be able to stop 'playing nice' with the rules of their society.

The Power of Indifference

One instigator of change is most curious: The Power of *Indifference.* Indifference is the power of no-power, but we need a deep, inner security to be truly indifferent to the whims of others.

In Victorian England, the new money allowed individuals to become indifferent to what others might think. In this way the person become free of the rules and the machine. When you no longer need the machine to feed and cloth you, it loses all power over you.

When you need the machine, you have to play 'nice'. You have to obey all the little rules of etiquette, say and do the right things, behave. The caveman only stopped hitting his neighbor with the club because his society instructed him to stop, and he needed that society - not because he came to an awareness of hitting another being wrong.

Look at Cain and Abel, a brother that murders his sibling! We NEED the rules to keep our primitive self in order, to stop our animal self running rampant.

Or so we are told.

Did Tarzan need the rules of English society? He got on perfectly well with his ape cousins, but he meets Jane, and his world is upended. For love he left the jungle, became 'civilized' and learned the rules of a new and very different society. Kindness changed him, not rules.

Here is where internal authority beats external rules. When we are governed by kindness and respect, there is little need for external rules. When we regard ourselves with kindness, our world shifts, and we find ourselves at the center of our being.

Opposing this is playing 'nice'. Playing 'nice' is a pretense that disconnects us from our true feelings. Playing 'nice' is really just obeying rules. Playing 'nice' is one of the nastiest things we can do to ourselves and others. Playing 'nice' is like saying "sorry" when you don't mean it.

Then came the 1960s

Society in the 1950s was as stratified as ever, but a huge shock was about to rock the Western cultures. The Beatles, the Stones, the fashion, the hippies, Woodstock: It represented the tumultuous overturning of everything, along with the jettisoning of all the rules. Be what you want to be, do what you want to do, yeah!

Free love and flowers in your hair! LSD and new horizons beckoned, and the rigid confines of the social order fell into pieces more surely than Humpty Dumpty. The conservative forces sought to rally, to fight back, but the boat of state was swamped by change. Vietnam shattered the illusions of war as being a good thing. Nixon destroyed the notion that the Government was a safe pair of hands. Rock and Roll threw out the sophistication of Jazz and installed the tribal rhythm that everyone could dance to.

Yet where did all that go? The brief flurry of freedom produced an amazing few decades, but go to a university today, and all you find are serious young people who want to get a decent job, and who would never do anything to upset their grades. The Mos Maiorum has re-established itself. The voice of independence lives on a few 'You Tube' channels and podcasts, but the concerns of the people are once more wrapped around buying the house, getting a raise, and saying what is considered appropriate. Social Media is a social quagmire. Politics continues as the lie it has always been. News is still the one eyed projection of a few media barons.

So what happened to the revolution? Well, for one, the middle classes got enslaved by debt during the price rises of the 1970s and beyond.

But the other obvious truth is that only a small group of people made the noise in the Sixties. It got a lot of coverage, a lot of people felt change was in the air, a few went along for the ride, but most stayed inside their sheltered world of should and should not. As the excitement faded, the old dinosaurs reared their ugly heads, and convention took hold, dropping the lead curtain of conformity over the small but exciting play that was the 1960s.

Does any body know what time it is? Does anybody really care? Chicago released the song in 1969, at the end of the era. It took till 1975 before the Vietnam War ended and by this time the price of fuel and commodities had soared. Petrol doubled, tripled, and quadrupled in price – the cost of living rocketed, the cost of housing began to soar. The fragile flower of the sixties was crushed underfoot by the hard heel of commerce, and debt swamped the middle classes.

Don't you DARE stand up and declare yourself as free!

The Paradox of Rules

The problem is a social addiction to being told what to do. And if you don't, you get ostracised. When we don't play by the accepted rules, no one wants you in their sandpit. If you are seen to be breaking or ignoring the mores of society, you will find yourself as an uninvited guest at every party you attend. You have to appear to be towing the line, you must 'play nice': which is fine, we all can smile and pretend, if we must.

But remember, this is precisely what psychopaths do.

Can you break rules and yet fit in? This depends on what rules you follow! I offer you the ultimate paradox, by following the Rat Rules, you can become free of rules!

OPPORTUNITY and LUCK are the TRUE GODS of your inner RAT. Respect these twin aspects of life and you will never go wrong.

SYMBOLS

We are run by symbols. They elicit a response within the unconscious, and this response effectively directs our lives. There are overt symbols, such as a national flag, or covert ones such as an ideal or a MEME impressed upon us.

Without word or thought, symbols convey deep meaning to the individual and the group. In modern America, the MAGA hat is a symbol. But what it means to one person is very different to what it means to another. To one person it means solidarity and setting the country to rights, to another, errant stupidity and the destruction of democracy.

Wearing a MAGA hat, placing the symbol on your body, signals you have joined a movement. You don't need anything but the hat to join this movement. It is the badge, the uniform, and the contract. By placing it on your head it means you have signed up. You are part of the team, the crew; you are one of the people who are changing America! And when you see another wearing the same, you are unified in this movement.

THIS is core to the power of symbols.

Flags are the symbol of a country, but what they MEAN is ownership. A Union Jack on a building means it is owned by Britain. The American Revolution pulled down the Union Jack and installed the Stars and Stripes. The United States now owned the country!

These are the OVERT symbols that control our world. Yet on a personal level, it is the small, apparently insignificant ones that rule us. In the UNCONSCIOUS there are many symbols we hold dear, and which own us. We see someone talking with our partner, so we trot up, smile, and put our arm around him or her: Supposedly we are signaling that we love and cherish that person. We are showing that we are together. The truth is more likely that we are placing a flag - we are saying this is MINE.

Small, insignificant actions like this, saying a person is OWNED, have so many flow on effects. You are placing boundaries over them, and yourself. You are not defining a relationship; you are confining it to a set of expectations. And what happens when you are locked in the same room as a person for too long? You start to hate each other.

Or maybe the person WANTS to be owned, it makes them feel secure. Who can say? But the SYMBOL is a keyhole into a world of meaning.

Ownership is a compulsion in Western Society. We feel we have to own in order to feel safe – it is not wrong, but where does it stop? Have you ever experienced the ball keeping neighbor? If the ball falls in their yard, kiss it goodbye - you are never seeing it again. They believe they are telling you their yard is out of bounds, but what they are actually saying is that they have no agreement with your society.

The yard is the symbol of their right to do as they damn well please, and tough if your ball goes in there. Righteous anger, ownership, these are SYMBOLS of a person cutting themselves off from a natural interaction with the world around them. And any person who willingly disconnects from their environment is doing so out of fear or loathing – Disconnection leads to suffering.

Isolation, loneliness, depression, and anxiety – conditions created by DISCONNECTION. And the reason for the disconnection will be some sort of buried symbol, or image, inside that person.

How do We Create Personal Symbols?

We create symbols out of ordinary events. Maybe the kid down the road gets a dart gun, and he shoots you with it. Well, maybe you never liked that child? Maybe you wanted a dart gun but never got one? Let's say you react to his aggression by keeping his dart. That dart is now YOURS, and he's not getting it back. So the child goes to his parents, they see your parents, and the kid gets his stupid dart back. You are not happy, but soon enough you forget about the dart.

Only, you didn't forgive and let it go, you buried the resentment you felt. This become a symbol.

Later in life, someone does you a small slight. Well, you now hold a grudge like you held that dart. There is no parent to force you to let it go. It's YOUR grudge; you are never giving it up.

Your wife tells you to stop being childish and let it go. No way – she can't tell you what to do. She's not your parent – who does she think she is?

Get it? The symbol buried in you has morphed into a grudge that controls your behavior. Unless you have a very astute parent, one who understands your thinking and recognizes how small seeds grow, then you will bury that dart incident in your subconscious as a SYMBOL, one that is otherwise called a KARMA - a picture that controls you.

Thus the supreme importance of Rule One: It's not about you. Take nothing personally: the dart was not about you. The fact he was lucky enough to get a dart gun and you weren't – it is not about YOU. The fact he shot you with it, it really wasn't about you, that kid had his own reasons for shooting you. He may have even thought it was a way to make you his friend!

Extend this thinking! What happens when you take offence over something?

If someone does or says anything that causes a reaction, then it is a clear sign that you have a buried symbol lodged inside your psyche. By presuming it is not about you, you stop feeding this Symbol with the power to affect you. If nothing else from this book, remember this simple fact: You CANNOT give offense. You can only TAKE it. Remember this, and you will save yourself a lot of pain and suffering.

You cannot GIVE offense to another – You can CAUSE it by striking someone, that IS an offense but even so, emotional offense is a thing another can only TAKE. You can be offensive with your behavior. You can be rude, nasty, and careless of another's feelings – but you cannot personally GIVE offense to another person unless you cross over and strike them physically.

If someone crosses the boundary, self-defense applies – but it is still not about you! It is his or her unresolved issues you are dealing with.

Rule One: *It's not about you.* Follow the bouncing ball of logic here: If it is not about you, you cannot take offense, can you? Sure, protect yourself. Protect your vulnerable spots. But here's the secret: When you KNOW it is not your problem, a certain sort of magic occurs.

You become a mirror! You reflect to that person what they are. They may get even more aggressive at this point, blaming you for their issues, accusing you of whatever. But when you know, deeply and earnestly, that it just is not about you, it is water off the ducks back. You attain a sort of immunity.

Forgiveness

Let's assume you DID take offense. You have a buried symbol in your psyche – a buried picture that accepts and takes in the energy being thrown at you - now, guess what? This action pierces the state of your being. It causes you emotional and mental hurt that feels absolutely real.

How do you escape this? Well, you forgive the person, you forgive yourself, and you move on. You are not approving their behavior, or your reaction, but you are letting it go so that YOU can carry on.

Forgiveness is releasing YOU from the karma, not them. It is arrogance to presume your forgiveness somehow improves THEM – It does not. It helps you get past the flaw inside yourself.

Let's take an extreme example, some murderer turns up and kills every member of your family. You hate them, you burn for revenge, how could they do this to them, to you? They are evil and deserve to die! This may well be true, they may be evil, they may well deserve to die, but holding to the hurt and pain only hurts you. It does nothing to harm them. You forgive so YOU can move on, so that you can get back to the space where you understand, it was never about you.

When you apply Rule One, what happens internally is that you start to unpack the code the symbols or Memes inside you were written with.

The code for the flag of your country, as one example, goes back to the foundations of your culture. Like computer software, the flag is a language used to describe to the computer how it should act, and in what instance it should perform this or that function.

When you understand that it is not about YOU, the pattern behind the things that built your persona, your beliefs, your sense of right and wrong – all this starts to reveal itself. I cannot express more deeply how important and how simple this principle is: It is not about you!

Which begs the question, what are you?

Take away the patterns trained into the mind, and what is left? Take away the emotions and beliefs you have incorporated into yourself, and what is left?

Imagine, because imagine is all you can do, that you are utterly free of everything. Imagine what you were before everything was put into and onto you! There you are, a baby. Imagine what it is like to be new born, or born again, as they say.

Being Born Again

"Unless a man be born again into the Kingdom of Heaven," and all that. But what does 'Born Again' mean? It is where Rule One, "It's not about You!" leads your consciousness. This liberates you from worldly concerns, it frees you from the shackles of ignorance, it strips the situation before you bare and you see the Emperor has no clothes.

When you see with the eyes of the newly born, everything is a discovery. Everything! Even the person shouting at you, it may feel terrible, but you have no guilt with which to blame yourself, or them, so you see it for what it is, anger.

You have discovered anger! When your mother wraps you up and feeds you, you have discovered Love! Everything is discovery.

Curiosity rules: The person before you turns into a thing to discover, not a thing to fear or blame or need - but a thing to understand.

Imagine your world this way RIGHT NOW. Now you realize all the 'stuff' you have been carrying, all your burdens, they are really tools of discovery. NOW, you can use your experience in this life as a tool to understand it better.

Being born again: Returning to the place from whence you first began, taking your natural innocence and forging it with experience. You have done it! Now what do you have? Power.

When you redirect your 'stuff' into discovery and curiosity, you attain the remarkable, unassailable power of perception.

The Touchani it was called, long ago. The Vedas call it Retumburra, the Wisdom of the Heart. The Tibetans call it the Vidya, the true seeing. There is a reason everyone has a name for it!

Perception is HOW you see, not what you see.

Slowly you turn round to face yourself – through the glass darkly, and then face to face. And what do you see? More importantly, HOW are you seeing your world?

Everything changes. You start to see the obvious beneath all things - you see through the dance of Maya, the illusions people wrap around themselves, and under all this you feel, sense, and know the dance of life.

And you truly understand that HOW you see is far more important than WHAT you see.

Symbols are constructed as an external exemplar of an ideal. The Flag is the exemplar of all that is good about a country; the forces behind the symbol that forged the flag are still there. Now you are seeing that it is not about YOU, you can begin to experience what is means.

I love the American Flag because of what it means: The breaking away from despotic rule, the act of self-determinism, the concept that all men are born equal (minus a little slavery) and the notion that the future is what we make it. It is all there in the flag.

I love the Australian flag, it carries the symbol of the Southern Cross with the Union Jack stuck into the corner. Some think it is wrong to have kept the British flag on there. Some believe the 'true' Australian flag is the simple Southern Cross flag of the failed revolution by the miners at the Eureka Stockade. This was a rebellion by gold miners over unfair tax, lack of representation, and the brutal rule of law where fairness to the miners was ignored. It symbolizes rebellion against the status quo and conformity to rules.

But the Australia Flag recognizes this - The Southern Cross is dominant over the British flag. While the British flag is itself a combination of the Irish, Scottish, and English flags. St George's Cross being the English flag, St Patrick's Cross, being the Irish flag, and St Andrew's Cross, being the Scottish flag.

Getting the Christian message here?

Underneath every symbol is a set of ideals, usually religious ideals. The settlement of the Americas was driven by a set of ideals. Freedom from religious tyranny drove the puritans to the new land. The invasion of England by the Vikings was driven by the need for land. (In the home country, only women could own land)

When you understand Rule One, you will see the core of the person attacking you: they are being driven by a set of misplaced ideals, and that these have little to do with you.

Everyone is being driven by an ideal or pain from their past. Everyone is obeying a sense of 'should' inside his or her psyche. But you can stop being the mouse on the wheel. How? It's not about YOU. Stop believing it is about you.

The Mystic Rat Says: If you make a mistake, don't just learn from it. USE IT! The Art of Living is all about recycling our negatives, by using them as paving stones.

Hop Down off the Cross

Symbols are the gestalt of a set of ideals and images. They are good and useful things to polarize a society and get it moving in a specific direction. They are tools that help a society define what it stands for and its reason for being. But when you take a symbol, such as Jesus dying on the cross for YOU, and make it YOURS you are potentially interfering with your own sense of who and what you are.

When you clutch the flag and say, "This is ME!" you are saying you belong to that country – yet you are lying to yourself. You are not your country. When you want to die for some grand ideal, you are lying to yourself. When you imagine you are better than your neighbor because they belong to a lesser club, have the wrong colored skin, etc. then you are lying to yourself.

Hop down off the cross! It is not about you! You are not a messiah who will save the world through your suffering. (AKA: Shoot the Pope)

Stop being run by the symbols and memes inside your heart and head. They are just pictures. Let it go, be brave enough to consider this one simple truth – NONE of it is about you.

What about ethics? There is nothing wrong with ethics, but they do not bring happiness, nor do they pay the rent. Ethics are needed for the safety of the society, and are a safety barrier to excess. But once we stop identifying with external notions of right and wrong, once we step back from being owned by our ideals, we start to see a new path open up – one that leads to freedom from the tyranny of self.

JUDGMENT

Veritas Nunquam Perit
(Truth Never Perishes)

People fear judgement. Our world is steeped in it, with others casting aspersions and gossip, judging you by their standards of right or wrong.

Someone walks in the room, and a little part of our mind starts adding up small details – we are judging with a thousand tiny little considerations about that person. Initially, this was a survival trait, something from our earliest times to ensure we recognized threat. Now, it is just a social habit.

The mental addition we come to with our internal dialogue is a judgment about that person. This is an endless trap that we fall into, and no one is immune. We are a society of judgers – not judges, but judgers. Yet we know our opinion counts for nothing! Our judgment has no value, while it hurts so many.

Because we feel powerless, we form into groups of agreement, cliques. If that the person walks in not wearing the right clothes, or saying the right thing, they are excluded from our circle.

The person entering that room often FEELS judged, and they will react to this.

As a Judge you have compared them against a myriad of criteria of what is acceptable, to determine if this right for you.

But as a JUDGER, you go a step further, and determine if THEY are right or wrong. You have broken Rule One and made this about YOU.

When a person obeys the Rat Rules, they can assess a situation in an entirely different way. When a person walks into a room, you judge if they are a threat or otherwise. If a threat, you take steps to cover yourself. Next: Do you wish to make friends, or not? Do they appear to be a person you can trust, or not?

You judge the SITUATION, not the person, and you CHOOSE your course. We are making a judgment, but not about the PERSON, we are judging the situation. Big difference.

You are being a JUDGE, not a JUDGER.

Living in a society as we do, we must judge situations, people, and our circumstances. We must weigh up considerations; take inventory of our assets and liabilities. We must judge whether a situation is a benefit or otherwise, or if this job is a better option than that job.

Accurate discrimination is based on HOW we see. Let's look at the Ladder of Logic behind this.

Logically: If our reasoning is faulty, our judgment will be faulty. Sound reason is therefore the basis of all good judgment.

However, our sense of reason is based on Logic: If our logic is faulty, our reasoning will be faulty.

Logic is based on perception. If how we see things is faulty, our logic is faulty.

Our judgments are therefore based on a train of considerations that are based on our perceptions. Which brings us back to determining HOW we see, not WHAT we see. We use logic and reasoning to come to a judgment, to find our place, but it is ALL based on HOW we see things.

So, what happens when we CHOOSE how we see things? Short answer: Every small detail of our entire life will change accordingly.

The Culture of Non-Judgment

In schools today there is a cult of 'non-judgment'. It sounds like a positive, but is it?

All cultures have a judge, a person appointed to judge others, usually for wrongdoing. Schools have seen fit to go the other way, to use perception and reasoning in a way that rewards everyone, not punish. The view is that children need positive reinforcement, not criticism, if they are to progress as productive members of society. If a child is coming last, you need to find a reason to encourage him, so you give him or her an award – maybe, "Best Eater of Lunch" or similar.

It is hard to find fault with such altruistic goals, and I completely agree on finding positives to encourage people. But sadly, the core perception this premise is based on is incorrect.

True judgment is neither positive nor negative: it is what it is. When we die, Osiris will weigh your heart against a feather, and you will be found wanting or otherwise. This 'judgment' is the sum total of your efforts in this life brought to focus.

You did this, it caused that, and here is your result. It is the basis of the math you are supposed to learn in school: *One plus one equals two.*

While the premise of reward over punishment sounds wonderful, you cannot avoid math. If the facts of a child's education (failing grades, poor attendance, etc.) results in him not graduating, his or her chances for a decent job, a good marriage, a happy life, are greatly diminished.

The PROBLEM with a 'no fail' system of constant reward is that a child no longer knows where they stand. Yes, they got an award for "Tries Hardest" but was that instead of a fail in Math, English, or Geography?

School ends, real life starts: What happens if a person can't add up properly? The world does not offer rewards for incompetence – the person who CAN add up gets the better job, the better pay, and the better life. Ergo, you suffer.

The Illusion of Positive Self-Esteem

Schools are promoting self-esteem. They seek to give the child a positive image of self. The Victorian Era ethic of punishment and reward is now seen as archaic and brutal. And it was!

On the surface, it is hard to find fault with this notion of improving a students self-esteem. I know mine suffered, I was caned every day in my Catholic boarding school for presumed wrongs. I would have had much better view of self if I was encouraged rather than constantly rebuked.

So how could this notion of building Self-Esteem possibly be wrong?

The mistake is made with the notion that self-esteem is more important than a correct assessment of your personal situation. It is not!

We have all seen the dreadful singer hop up for auditions on American Idol – they are truly awful, but all they have been given was positive reinforcement by a parent, or whoever. They have no idea how terrible they are.

Now the person is shattered, destroyed. Worse, they had not developed the strength to carry the weight of a critical assessment – and the cameras LOVE it. They focus in on the failing singer, and the anger that results from the critique – We hear the blame handed to the judges, how awful they are, how terrible they are for being so cruel, etc.

The irony: The person judged as being unworthy for a TV show harshly judges the judges for judging them so harshly.

Obviously, they were picked to audition because they were so terrible and didn't know it.

Unless our self-esteem is based on achievement, results, and meeting required standards, it is a dream. When a school or parent encourages failure as an option by calling it success, we train the person to be useless. And far worse than all of this, when we cosset a person in cotton wool thinking, we destroy their ability to fight back against adversity. *They can now not fail to fail!*

The Justice Trap

I spoke with a Jewish fellow who lives on Manhattan Island. He spent his days painting scenes of Central Park, and I asked him how he afforded living in New York, just doing what he pleased. He explained that he came from a wealthy family, but that he had no desire for business or pursuing the trappings of prestige.

His family owned the apartment, and gave him a small stipend. His only obligation was to turn up for family events, a thing he willingly accepted.

As a curiosity, I asked, "Why are the Jewish people so successful? Wherever they go, no matter the land or the circumstances, they do well."

"Oh, not all do well," he stressed. "Imagine what an awful situation I would be in if I didn't have a family to back me? But I do, and that is part of the reason we succeed as a people.

"But the real reason for the success of the Jewish people is very simple, we do not trust governments, nor do we expect fairness. This is a cultural thing and because of it, we own our own shops, our own farms, and our own banks. We do not trust that life will be fair, so we even the odds as much as we can."

Most people do not think like this. They live their lives expecting that there is some sort of scale measuring out justice and balancing things with fairness. Perhaps in the long term this is true, but in the short term, no. It is not that there is no justice; karma is real. The point is it is not up to you to administer it, nor to rely on it.

It is not our job to ensure everyone gets justice. It is not our job to save the world. It is not our job to determine what is right or wrong for another.

Likewise, it is not our job to protect someone from the results of their own actions.

When a school arbitrarily starts to take on the well being of the child as their purpose, they are failing in their purpose as a school. Their job is to educate. You CAN educate in a way that is gentle and uplifting, but to cosset a child's failings in terms of rewards is a nonsense.

When we place ourselves in a position of determining what is right for another, we break the Law of Non-Interference. We set ourselves up not as a Judge, but as a Pope. This is the danger of the Justice Trap. It is part of the cotton wool thinking we have inherited from media and Facebook.

Cotton Wool Thinking

The core of most problems in a person's life is faulty thinking. In "Your Erroneous Zones" Dr Wayne Dwyer targets the core of this cotton wool thinking. The book sold over Thirty Five Million copies, so it clearly spoke to a lot of people. He said something strikingly obvious about self worth – *If you rely on others for your validation, what you get is "other worth" not self-esteem.*

When a school seeks to improve your self-esteem by not paying attention to failure, they are undermining it. By offering approval without basis, they are removing the basis for approval in your life. The job of the school is to educate the child. That is it – that is the function. If that school churns out uneducated children, then they have FAILED. But wait, failure is so harsh: let's give the school an award for the, "Best Waste of Government Funding!"

You do not have to cane a child to communicate they are failing in any given area. You do not have to reward them to cosset their feelings. You just tell them the truth; gently, but as it is. Then let them rise to the occasion, or not.

To create false rewards to protect a person against failure is to train them in lies and deception. The basis of all good judgment in life is found in seeing things clearly, and obfuscating reality, supplanting it with cotton wool thinking, serves no one and gains nothing.

Finding the Truth

To find the truth inside ourselves, we have to cease judging. We have to cease weighing the scales, and comparing ourselves to others. We have to find the still, certain point within where everything is as it is. This is sanctuary; this is the Omphalos, the belly button of existence.

This state of BEING does not oppose judging situations or people, it just does not need it. Yes, you still need a sense of discrimination, but this is not comparison - it is asking if what is before you is a way to come to a point of balance, within which rests your place of being.

The Rat Rules are designed to help you reach this place. Let us recap and discover why they help, and how they help.

The first five are Internal Guidelines – suggestion on how to maintain the INNER self.

1. It's not About You

The first rule: It's not about you. This is central to the entire state of being the Greeks described as the Omphalos – the place of first becoming. By not being drawn into the arguments and comparisons of the world, you remain where you are, still and certain in your place.

2. Do not Should in your Own Nest

All the social training, all the upbringing you received, it is about what you SHOULD do. It is designed to keep society in order and the 'should' is the basis of all civilized behavior. But when you are entirely contained within yourself, you have no need for any "shoulds". You are free of them, thus free to act as you choose. The moment you incur a 'should' you raise prison bars around self.

3. Keep One Eye open

Being contained within self does not preclude the reality of predators – In the modern world, this is mostly people who want what you have. You do not need to stare at the world with your full attention, but you need to keep an awareness of the possibility of things going wrong. One foot in heaven, the other on earth, in other words.

4. Ask no Favors (Do not a beggar nor borrowers be)

Being self-contained means you reduce your level of debts to others and society. Credit for necessities, cash for luxuries is the golden rule. Beggars can't be choosers, they say? This is true. Equally true: Choosers can't be beggars

5. Keep your Teeth Honed (Be Prepared)

This follows on from all the previous guidelines. Keep an awareness of your external environment. Protect against the elements of change and of society. Always be prepared for a fight, even as you do everything to avoid it. By being prepared to fight, you create an aura of strength that most will shy away from.

The next three guidelines are "external" – they are how you defend against external adversity. While it is not about you, your survival and that of your loved ones may well depend on an understanding of the next three principles.

6. Have a Bolt Hole

In all things, the possibility of loss exists. Preparing for loss means to have a bolt hole, an escape plan in place. This can be as simple as cultivating friendships and associations with others, or as complex as equipping a cave in the mountains in case of nuclear war.

7. Do not Expose your Vulnerabilities

Predators exist. If someone wants what you have it is best not to present them with the opportunity to take it. This also means knowing what is valuable, and knowing what is worth protecting. EG: Gossip can undermine our standing in society. We need to protect our good name, but that is not defending vanity, it is maintaining the perception others have of us. If others have a negative view on our person, it can make it difficult to survive in that society.

8. Pay Attention to your Brother's Activity (but not their business)

In any given society we rub shoulders with many people. It pays to remain aware of their situation. If a person is looking morose and depressed they may act out of character, become aggressive, suicidal, etc. Or they are looking like a thief. Or they have gotten religion and are trying to convert people. If a person knows they are seen, they will be more circumspect in any action against you.

The last two guidelines are entirely personal. They describe the behavior of a successful person. You cannot be a success if you act like a failure, and the following guidelines speak on how to be the best person you can be.

9. Pick up and Dust Off

Things go wrong. We fall over, so we pick ourselves up and we dust off the problems. But this also means looking for jewels in the dust – pick them up, dust them off, and discover a greater wealth. This is an attitude of opening the heart, of allowing life to bring us joy and wealth.

10. Shoot the Pope

This is essential for happiness. We all like to have a positive self-image, but most of the ideals we presume to be 'positive' are the hidden memes of society. We have nothing to prove, no one to impress. Kill that pompous self, let it die. Accept yourself, as you are, warts and all. You cannot find freedom with the burden of self importance on your shoulders.

ALL the above is about protecting the still certain point within. In this place the silent voice speaks, gently guiding you through the twists and turns of life.

Alone with all my selves, I contemplate: Loves, hates, inbetweens, they are all there in my book.

IN CLOSING

The notion of the Mystic Rat, the King Rat, and Ratology started as a way to lessen the angry voices on the Usenet groups of the mid 1990s. In those early days of the net, opinions became inflamed very easily, and arguments over what amounted to very little were commonplace. I would seek to lighten the conversation by inserting "Wise Old Indian" saying, but saying it was the Lord High Rat speaking.

It caught people's attention and took their mind off the argument, perhaps to laugh, or perhaps to ridicule myself for saying such nonsense – but it didn't matter – things cooled, and people could discuss things more easily.

More than a few souls suggested I put the "wise sayings" into a book, and eventually I did, using the term Ratology. The word RAT, for the Reality Awareness Trigger, comes out of the RAS – the Reticulation Activating System – the central part of the brain responsible for regulating awareness. The "Ology" is the study of how to find this instinctual awareness: Rat-ology.

I called it a 'genuinely artificial religion', a tongue in cheek term that came from a can of beans from the USA that proudly proclaimed it contained, "Genuine artificial bacon pieces!".

Religion means to "re-tie" or "reconnect" in Latin. This is appropriate as practicing the Rat Rules will (ideally) help you to reconnect the inner child with the outer adult.

I called it : Ratology: Way of the Un-Dammed.

This study is a way to LIVE life. Practice the Rat Rules and you will never arrive at old age regretting your decisions, or bemoaning your outcomes.

It is a path of wakefulness: eyes open to greet the moment, breathing in deep to take as much of it as you can. Specifically, it is a way to live as an expression of self, rather than the repression of self that the rules of society (essentially) teach us.

Why "Un-Dammed"? There is no martyr's curse hanging over your head, no threat of eternal damnation – but most are dammed up with conformity and energy they have not allowed to flow. The Way of the Rat is really just a way to release inhibitions, to become Un-Dammed. It is a free flowing experience that carries a will and a wish to live fully, embracing all that comes.

It all boils down to HOW we see. Specifically: the ability to alter how we see things. The ability to shift our viewpoint means we are in charge of our mind and imagination. This allows us a clearer view, which leads to freedom.

Life is for living. When this song becomes the core of our perception, everything works out better for us and for those around us. So, I will leave you with "Life is for Living" as a mantra. Use it to focus on what is important in your life: LIVING.

WHO GIVES A RATS
An Expose Into the Nature of Being Human

A working manual that shows you how
to stop doing what you "should" and
instead, start being who you ARE

Ecallaw Leachim

RATOLOGY II

Did you enjoy The Rat Rules? Go for ROUND TWO!

Book Two is now available on Amazon. Explore the deep patterns that control
every person and learn to renegotiate your agreement with life.

Available on Amazon

Be a VICTOR, not a VICTIM!

To a spider, the fly in the web is not a victim, it is food. When it is finished being food, it is dead and it is useless. Does this make spiders cruel? No, they are just hungry, like everyone. The real message is simple: If your mentality is that of a poor week helpless thing, then you will look like food to the carnivore.

Your inner Rat is what awakens you to the webs of deceit and lies woven all around you. These things are webs - designed to catch your attention, to hypnotize you, and make you supper. But when you listen to your Rat, you will see the trap, thus you won't be the spiders next meal.

There are no victims, there are only those who did not listen to, or understand, their inner whispers. And if you are not a victim, what are you?

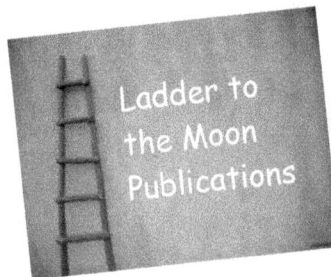

Ladder to
the Moon
Publications

www.laddertothemoon.com.au

Aiming for the Stars is much easier if we stop off at the Moon. We are then out of the atmosphere of our past, and can see things more clearly. We are lighter, can jump higher and further than ever before, and it takes far less energy to start each journey.

The hard part is climbing that Ladder to the Moon.

The RAT RULES - ISBN: 978-0-6452723-7-6

Fly Free
Let the Burdens Fall

Traversing life can seem an arduous task. We have to cross that field of stones, trying to find our way, often feeling sorry for ourselves.
We have a choice: Let go, or hold on. If we let go of our precious notions, we grasp that it is not about ourselves. Or we hold onto our misery and go another round on the Wheel of Becoming - the Awagawan.
This is the name for the Wheel of Karma. This is the central point of our suffering. This is why we can't have nice things.
Poverty, unhappiness, low esteem, lack of self respect - this is all part of the wheel.
How do you escape this trap? You can start by not putting yourself at the center of the wheel! If isn't about YOU! You don't need a sense of importance!

Once you release this last little vanity, once you grasp it is not about YOU, you are set free from the prison of your past, and can use its bricks to construct the palace of your future.

About the Author

Little can be said of the author other than he is a complete rat who likes poker. Otherwise, he has raised the children, done the divorce, fed the cats, played with the dog, buried the dead fish, and generally had a life like most people.
Aside from writing, he is a musician, healer, and inventor.
Ecallaw Leachim is an Australian, raised in New Guinea for a time and brought up by such a strict Catholic mother that he actually ASKED to be sent to Boarding School. Prison, he quipped, was the other option not open to him at the time.
If you loved this book, don't just write and tell him, please REVIEW the book on Amazon.
If you hated it, well give it time.

The **BLACK** ART of HOLDEM

Appeasing the Poker Gods by.

Reading the O.D.D.S
Building OPPORTUNITY
Creating YOUR LUCK

Don't just PLAY Holdem!
WIN the Damn Game!
Make MONEY from it!

Ecallaw "Ratty" Leachim

The Author made a living playing poker. You can too!

"An incredible insight into the psychology and practice of playing Holdem."

Available on Amazon

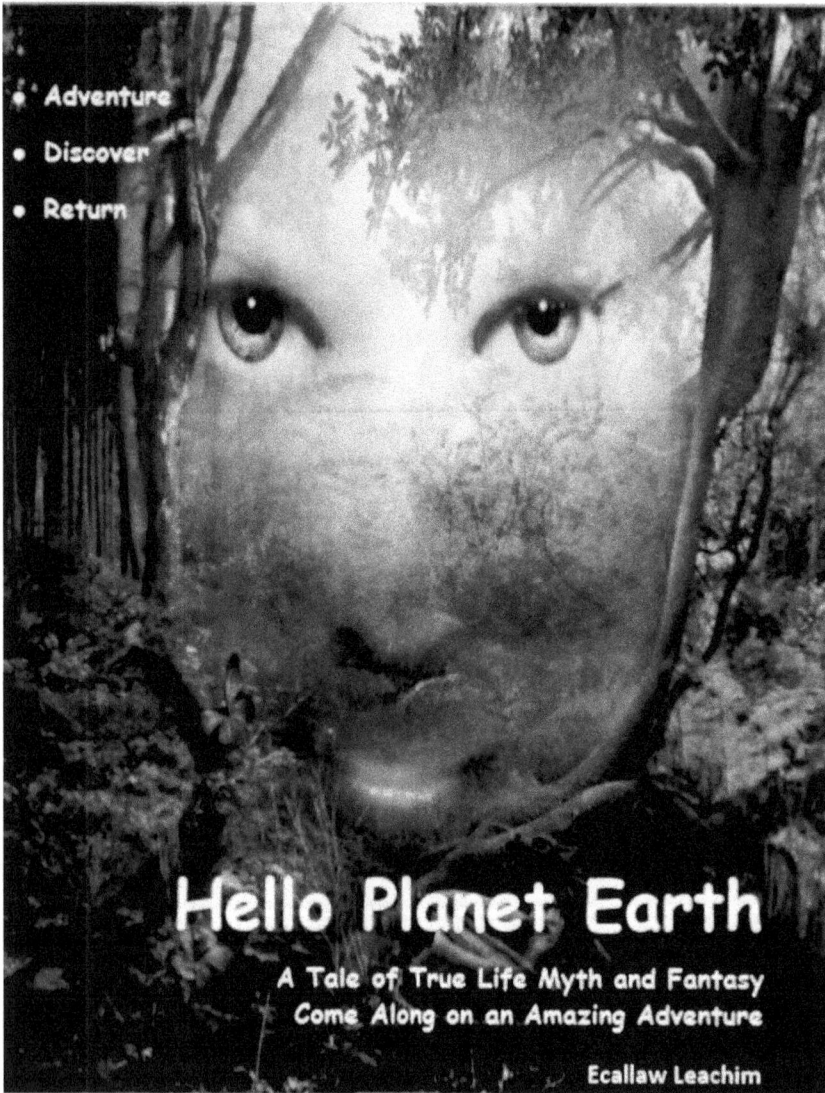

- Adventure
- Discover
- Return

Hello Planet Earth

A Tale of True Life Myth and Fantasy
Come Along on an Amazing Adventure

Ecallaw Leachim

"An Absolute Delight"
T.C. Sydney

It was time to make the journey, to leave behind the happenstance of the day to day, and discover a new world out in the forest.

The author wrote this book in the 1980s, when he was on deaths door.

It is an amazing and delightful experience that will put a smile on your face.

Available on Amazon

The WAND

Waking the Dragon

Ecallaw Leachim

Utterly delightful.
This book collapses
the dimensions
between the human
and all other realms.
A delight from start
to finish.

Available on Amazon

www.ingramcontent.com/pod-product-compliance
Lightning Source LLC
Chambersburg PA
CBHW061955090426
42811CB00006B/937